Lanuco River

CITLALTÉPETL
(18,700 feet)

• **Mexico City**

POPOCATÉPETL (17,887 feet)

• Puebla

YUCATÁN

PENINSULA

ISTHMUS

OF

TEHUANTEPEC

MADRE DEL SUR

SIERRA

MADRE DE CHIAPAS

MEXICO

MEXICO

By the Editors of Time-Life Books
with photographs by Pedro Meyer and Graciela Iturbide

TIME-LIFE BOOKS ∘ ALEXANDRIA, VIRGINIA

TIME-LIFE BOOKS

This volume is one in a series of books describing countries of the world, their lands, peoples, histories, economies and governments.

For information on and a full description of any of the Time-Life Books series listed above, please call 1-800-621-7026 or write:
Reader Information
Time-Life Customer Service
P.O. Box C-32068
Richmond, Virginia 23261-2068

THE COVER: The face of the sun-god Tonatiuh stares enigmatically from the center of Mexico's greatest Aztec relic, the 26 ton Calendar Stone. Now housed in Mexico City's National Museum of Anthropology, the stone takes its name from the inscriptions surrounding the face, which define the Aztec division of the year into 18 months of 20 days each.

PAGES 1 and 2: The eagle-like bird shown on page 1 has been the emblem of Mexico since 1823. The emblem appears on the nation's flag *(page 2)*.

ENDPAPERS: With most of its 759,529 square miles of territory made up of mountain ranges and plateaus, Mexico sits high and dry. The average altitude is 3,500 feet; 70 percent of the country is semi-arid. The triangles on the back endpaper map indicate principal archeological sites.

Time-Life Books Inc.
is a wholly owned subsidiary of

TIME INCORPORATED

FOUNDER: Henry R. Luce 1898-1967

Editor-in-Chief: Henry Anatole Grunwald
President: J. Richard Munro
Chairman of the Board: Ralph P. Davidson
Corporate Editor: Ray Cave
Group Vice President, Books: Reginald K. Brack Jr.
Vice President, Books: George Artandi

TIME-LIFE BOOKS INC.

EDITOR: George Constable
Executive Editor: George Daniels
Editorial General Manager: Neal Goff
Director of Design: Louis Klein
Director of Editorial Resources: Phyllis K. Wise
Editorial Board: Dale M. Brown, Roberta R. Conlan, Ellen Phillips, Gerry Schremp, Donia Ann Steele, Rosalind Stubenberg, Kit van Tulleken, Henry Woodhead
Director of Research and Photography: John Conrad Weiser

PRESIDENT: William J. Henry
Senior Vice President: Christopher T. Linen
Vice Presidents: Stephen L. Bair, Edward Brash, Ralph Cuomo, Robert A. Ellis, John M. Fahey Jr., Juanita T. James, James L. Mercer, Wilhelm R. Saake, Robert H. Smith, Paul R. Stewart, Leopoldo Toralbolla

LIBRARY OF NATIONS

SERIES DIRECTOR: Dale M. Brown
Designer: Ray Ripper
Chief Researcher: Barbara S. Levitt

Editorial Staff for *Mexico*
Associate Editors: Anne Horan, David S. Thomson (text); Jane Speicher Jordan (pictures)
Researchers: Rita Thievon Mullin (principal), Paula York-Soderlund
Copy Coordinators: Margery duMond, Robert M. S. Somerville
Picture Coordinator: Renée DeSandies, Erin Monroney
Editorial Assistant: Myrna E. Traylor

Special Contributors: The chapter texts were written by: Ronald H. Bailey, William Weber Johnson, Gordon Mott, Philip W. Payne, Bryce Walker and Gail Cameron Wescott.
Other Contributors: Ann Kuhns Corson, William Forbis, Martha R. George, Rosemary George, Kenneth E. Hancock (design), Martin Mann and Milton Orshefsky.

Editorial Operations
Copy Chief: Diane Ullius
Editorial Operations: Caroline A. Boubin (manager)
Production: Celia Beattie
Quality Control: James J. Cox (director)
Library: Louise D. Forstall

Correspondents: Elisabeth Kraemer-Singh (Bonn); Dorothy Bacon (London); Miriam Hsia, Lucy T. Voulgaris (New York); Maria Vincenza Aloisi, Josephine du Brusle (Paris); Ann Natanson (Rome). Valuable assistance was also provided by: Susan Masuoka (Mexico City); Carolyn Chubet, Christina Lieberman (New York).

Assistant Editor for the U.S. edition: Karin Kinney

CONSULTANTS

Michael D. Coe, professor of anthropology at Yale University, has written extensively about the ancient cultures of Mexico. Guillermo de la Peña, an anthropologist, teaches at the Center for Anthropological Studies at the College of Michoacán, Zamora, Michoacán, Mexico. George W. Grayson, author of *The Politics of Mexican Oil,* is professor of government at the College of William and Mary, Williamsburg, Virginia. Lydia D. Hazera lectures on Latin American literature at George Mason University, Fairfax, Virginia. Michael C. Meyer, co-author of *The Course of Mexican History,* is director of the Latin American Center at the University of Arizona, Tucson. Victor Sorell, born in Mexico, teaches Chicano, Mexican and Latin American art history at Chicago State University.

PHOTOGRAPHERS

Pedro Meyer and Graciela Iturbide, who live in Mexico City, spent eight weeks traveling through Mexico shooting pictures for this book. Their photographs of Mexican life have been exhibited at home and abroad and have appeared in numerous international publications.

Printed in U.S.A.
Published simultaneously in Canada.
School and library distribution by Silver Burdett Company, Morristown, New Jersey.

TIME-LIFE is a trademark of Time Incorporated U.S.A.

Library of Congress Cataloging in Publication Data
Main entry under title:
Mexico.
  (Library of nations)
  Bibliography: p.
  Includes index.
  1. Mexico. I. Time-Life Books. II. Series: Library of Nations (Alexandria, Va.)
F1208.M5827 1986   972   85-29679
ISBN 0-8094-5128-X
ISBN 0-8094-5129-8 (lib. bdg.)

In Spanish usage, surnames are usually formed with the father's name first, followed by the mother's maiden name. Generally, the first surname is the only one used as in the case of the writer Carlos Fuentes. In some instances, to distinguish among common names, both surnames are used, as for former president José López Portillo.

CONTENTS

EXPLOITING AN ANCIENT RESOURCE

As this chart shows, Mexico is the world's leading silver producer, with Peru and the Soviet Union in second and third place. By contrast, the 10 nations of the European Economic Community together produce only 1.5 percent of the world output.

Since the arrival of the Spaniards more than 400 years ago, an estimated $1.2 trillion dollars' worth of the metal has been extracted from Mexican ore. More than 475 large and small silver producers operate today, some dating back to colonial times. The most important of these — indeed, the world's largest mine — opened in 1982 and can produce nine million troy ounces a year. Mexico's present annual output of close to 64 million troy ounces can be expected to rise in response to improved silver prices.

PERCENTAGE OF WORLD SILVER OUTPUT

15

10

5

MEXICO   PERU   U.S.S.R.   EUROPEAN ECONOMIC COMMUNITY

Once the country's richest city, the mining town of Guanajuato still produces 8 percent of Mexico's silver. At right is a statue of El Pipila, a local hero. During

6

the struggle for independence from Spain, he singlehandedly attacked the Guanajuato granary, where the Spaniards had holed up, and set it afire.

AN OLD LAND OF YOUNG PEOPLE

More than half of Mexico's population of 79 million is under the age of 20, a startling statistic. But perhaps more startling is the fact that nearly three quarters of the Mexicans are under 30. The country today has nearly four times as many people as in 1940.

Why this acceleration in population growth? Rapid economic and social development in the last half century stimulated the flow of poor from the countryside into the cities, where improved sanitation, health facilities and education helped reduce mortality rates, especially among infants. In terms of employment, so many Mexicans are being added to the work force that 800,000 new jobs must be created annually just to keep up with the expanding labor pool.

PERCENTAGE OF POPULATION

0–9
10–19
20–29
30–39
40–49
50–59
60+

10

20

30

Sixteen members strong, this Otomí Indian family consists of three generations living in one home. The mother and father at center have eight children of

their own, ranging in age from 6 to 28, as well as three grandchildren.

In a photograph taken from a parasail, the towrope of which can be seen at left, Pacific waves wash the beach at Puerto Vallarta, one of Mexico's premier

AN INDUSTRY BASED ON PLEASURE

Few countries offer more to travelers than Mexico, with its sunny beaches, mountain scenery, colorful towns, ancient ruins and vibrant culture. Not surprisingly, tourism is one of Mexico's major industries; in the early 1980s, it generated revenues of almost $1.5 billion a year and provided jobs for 650,000 people.

In recognition of the industry's importance to the economy, the government gave cabinet-level status to the Department of Tourism in 1974. The department takes pains to ensure that facilities are maintained and new ones built, but in so doing it has provoked criticism in some quarters. There are those who feel that in catering to fun-seeking foreigners, the government is tying up funds and energies that might be better used in improving the lot of poor Mexicans.

resorts. Only a couple of decades ago Puerto Vallarta was an inaccessible fishing village; now it is visited by thousands of sun worshippers.

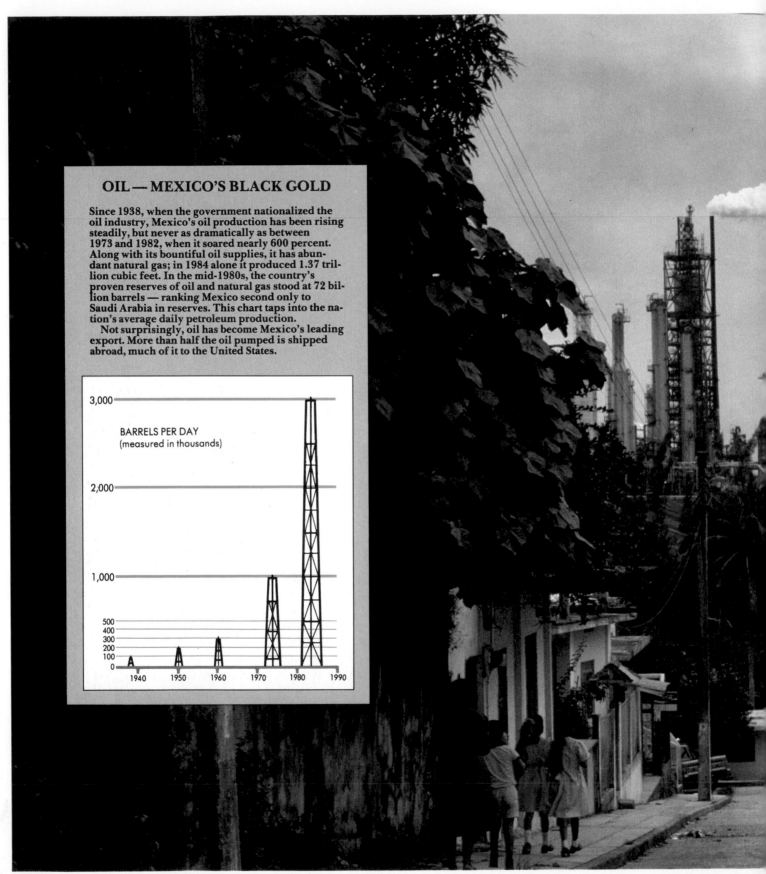

OIL — MEXICO'S BLACK GOLD

Since 1938, when the government nationalized the oil industry, Mexico's oil production has been rising steadily, but never as dramatically as between 1973 and 1982, when it soared nearly 600 percent. Along with its bountiful oil supplies, it has abundant natural gas; in 1984 alone it produced 1.37 trillion cubic feet. In the mid-1980s, the country's proven reserves of oil and natural gas stood at 72 billion barrels — ranking Mexico second only to Saudi Arabia in reserves. This chart taps into the nation's average daily petroleum production.

Not surprisingly, oil has become Mexico's leading export. More than half the oil pumped is shipped abroad, much of it to the United States.

BARRELS PER DAY
(measured in thousands)

Acrid smoke billows across the sky in the oil town of Minatitlán, near Mexico's southern Gulf Coast. Minatitlán, one of the country's largest refining

12

and petrochemical centers, processes 200,000 barrels of crude oil a day, shipping it via pipeline and tanker to various domestic and overseas markets.

The bounty of the Mexican earth fills bins at a market in the town of Juchitán, in Oaxaca. Although the number of agricultural workers has been going

14

A DRAMATIC SHIFT IN THE WORK FORCE

Industrialization and a growth in the service area of the economy have proceeded rapidly in Mexico since midcentury *(graph at right)*. This has produced a significant shift in the distribution of the labor force, reflecting the transition from a rural, agriculturally based economy to an urban, industrialized and service-oriented one typical of developed nations. As unemployed countryfolk have fled to the cities in search of jobs, the rural proportion of the population has shrunk. In 1950 farm workers accounted for 62.4 percent of the labor force; in 1980 they were 37.4 percent; and by the turn of the century they should make up only 17.8 percent.

PERCENTAGE OF WORK FORCE

60
50
40
30
20
10

AGRICULTURE

SERVICES

INDUSTRY

1950   1980   2000

down, agricultural production has been increasing dramatically since the introduction of modern farming methods.

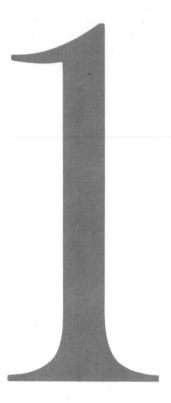

Two children and their dog watch over laundry set out on a maguey plant to dry. Although Mexico is industrializing, old ways persist — and so do old problems. "Awash with oil, Mexico has not found solutions to poverty, hunger, malnutrition, income inequalities," notes one student of Mexican affairs.

A LAND OF VIOLENT CONTRASTS

Every day, just after sunup, a squad of smartly uniformed soldiers emerges from the ornate National Palace and marches to the very center of the Plaza of the Constitution, or Zócalo, Mexico City's main square. While a band plays, one of the soldiers raises a green, white and red flag bearing in its center panel the emblem of a taloned bird perching on a cactus and clutching a snake in its sharp beak. A new day has officially begun in Mexico.

Before the day is done, thousands of the city's 2.4 million motor vehicles — from chauffeur-driven limousines to rattletrap pickup trucks — will have eddied fiercely around the Zócalo, honking impatiently and jockeying for position. Diplomats and dark-suited businessmen with briefcases will have hurried in and out of the National Palace to confer with government officials regarding oil concessions and peso exchange rates. Unemployed *campesinos,* peasants from the countryside, will have squatted along one end of the Zócalo, hawking their services, some using hand-lettered signs to advertise their skills. And a choking smog will have moved down from the northern edge of the city, where the industrial zone and most of the capital's 130,000 factories and workshops are located.

Such juxtapositions of the new and the old, of formality and disorder, of wealth and poverty, are the very soul of Mexico. The military ceremony as such is modern, but the flag's emblem is the symbol of the Aztec civilization, which neither 300 years of Spanish colonial rule nor four decades of postwar industrialization have altogether obscured. The vehicles and the smog reflect Mexico's entry into the industrial world, but the squatters and the shoeshine boys reflect its inability to keep its citizens employed.

The same scene is played out all through Mexico. In other cities, Spanish colonial bell towers and colonnaded mansions crowd against sleek skyscrapers, and narrow cobbled streets empty into broad macadamized boulevards. In the countryside, horse-drawn plows till the fields, but many a young farmer wears a visored cap advertising foreign farm equipment, a T-shirt touting an American baseball team and a black plastic wrist watch imported from Japan. And for all the modernity of his appearance he will still faithfully take part in the rituals of ancient festivals.

Mexico's contrasts are the result of a rich and complex cultural heritage in which Indian and Spanish roots are tangled, a vast geographical terrain that spans 759,529 square miles, and a late entry into the world of social and technological innovation. Only in the wake of the Mexican revolution, which racked the country from 1910 to 1920, did the government take practical measures toward social equality. And only in World War II, when wartime shortages in the United States and Europe deprived Mexico of imports on which it had come to depend, did the country begin to industrialize in earnest. "For the first time in our history," wrote the Mexican scholar and diplomat Octavio Paz soon after the war, "we are contemporaries of all mankind."

Ever since, Mexico has been hurrying to catch up with its contemporaries and to play a role with them in international affairs. But it wants to do so without discarding the cultural traditions that make the nation unique and give it reasons for taking pride in its own idiosyncrasies.

Mexico is the world's largest Spanish-speaking nation (it has a population in excess of 79 million, while Spain itself counts only 38 million). Educated Mexicans make the claim that they speak the purest Spanish anywhere in the Western Hemisphere; only Colombians rival them in command of the mother tongue. But some among their countrymen speak *pocho;* the descriptive term can be translated literally as "discolored" or "faded." When used with respect to language, *pocho* means a slangy mixture of Spanish and English (a result of the frequent showing of American movies and television programs, of Mexicans' crossing the border as migrant workers and of the Americans' coming south as tourists). An estimated 3.5 million Mexicans still cling to Náhuatl, the Aztec language spoken before the Spaniards' arrival, and another 2.5 million speak one of 55 other surviving Indian tongues.

Regardless of tongue and regardless of social and economic standing, the Mexican is a study in contrasts. Foreigners sometimes see Mexicans as simultaneously haughty and apologetic, courteous and rude, shy and assertive. Or they emphasize the tougher of those contrasts and look upon the Mexican character as quintessentially *macho,* a Spanish word strictly meaning "male" or "masculine" but in cultural terms connoting something more.

"One word sums up the aggressiveness, insensitivity, invulnerability and other attributes of the *macho,*" wrote Octavio Paz: "power. It is force without

the discipline of any notion of order: arbitrary power, the will without reins and without a set course. The essential attribute of the *macho* — power — almost always reveals itself as a capacity for wounding, humiliating, annihilating. We instinctively regard the world around us to be dangerous," Paz went on, writing of the Mexicans. "This reaction is justifiable if one considers what our history has been and the kind of society we have created. The harshness and hostility of our environment, and the hidden, indefinable threat that is always afloat in the air, oblige us to close ourselves in, like those plants that survive by storing up liquid within their spiny exteriors."

The land is as diverse and contrary as the people who live on it. To judge from a map *(front endpaper)*, it would seem to be made up of ill-fitting parts, as if fragments of earth had drifted together willy-nilly. And that is just about what happened.

Mexico is situated at the juncture of three of the tectonic plates that make up the earth's crust. Those three plates — the North American Plate, the Caribbean Plate and the Cocos Plate, which lies underneath the Pacific Ocean — arrived more or less in their present neighborhood hundreds of millions of years ago, but they are chronically restless. During eons of colliding and slipping under and over one another's edges, they have ignited volcanoes, built mountains and convulsed the land with earthquakes. Through the long course of geological history, they have helped to give Mexico a legacy of terrain, plant life and climate as complex as any on the planet.

The topography defies easy summation. When the conquistador Hernán Cortés was asked by King Charles V of Spain to describe the lay of the land, he was at a loss for words — goes the story — and so he crumpled a piece of paper and tossed it onto the table before the monarch.

Cortés' graphic presentation was essentially correct. Mexico's only lowlands occur in narrow bands running in interrupted strips along the east and west coasts, and in the Yucatán Peninsula, a shield of limestone that is much like the floor of the adjacent sea.

For the rest, Mexico is craggy and high. Almost 70 percent lies at more than 1,500 feet above sea level, and some mountains reach towering heights of 15,000 feet and more. Much of it consists of a great highland plateau, called the Meseta Central, which comes down from the high plains of Texas and New Mexico in the north and is rimmed on the west, east and south by mountains.

The northern part of the highland area, at an elevation of about 3,000 feet above sea level, is made up of broad basins with salt-saturated floors that are hospitable only to certain grasses and scrubby trees. At the southern end of the plateau is the region known as Central Mexico; here is the hub of the nation's politics, economy and population. This area, too, is composed of basins, but they lie higher (at elevations of 5,000 to 8,000 feet) than those of the north, and the land is less desiccated than that of the north.

Mexico's mountains constitute four major chains: the Sierra Madre Occidental, the Sierra Madre Oriental, the Sierra Madre del Sur and the Sierra Madre de Chiapas. The first two of these, which originate in the American Sierra Nevada and Rocky Mountains respectively, run roughly parallel to the west and east coasts of Mexico, until they converge in Central Mexico, about at the site of Mexico City. The third range, the Sierra Madre del Sur, runs along the southwestern coast through Guerrero and into Oaxaca; and the fourth, the Sierra Madre de Chiapas, runs from the state of Chiapas south into Guatemala.

Where the two northern chains come together, in a band running from east to west, sits the region of greatest seismic activity. Tremors are frequent and

In a candlelit scene, Mexican villagers crowd the gravesites of a cemetery on November 2, Day of the Dead. Families honor their departed by bringing them food and flowers; tradition holds that the deceased are granted hearing and appetite for the day.

1

sometimes calamitous; a series of earthquakes in 1957 took 60 lives in Mexico City and caused $25 million in property damage. In 1985, a more devastating earthquake there killed 20,000 people and destroyed hundreds of buildings, leaving 50,000 people homeless. Large structures built on pilings to flex with the earth tremors withstood the quake for the most part. But tall buildings standing near each other vibrated at different frequencies and collided, causing smaller buildings to collapse. Adobe slum houses simply fell apart.

In this geologically unstable zone are found the greatest of the volcanoes, and these are also a matter of deep concern. Some, such as Citlaltépetl, Popocatépetl, Iztaccíhuatl, Jorullo and Colima, have been periodically active ever since the time of the Aztecs (in their language, Popocatépetl meant "smoking mountain" and Iztaccíhuatl "white woman"). At least one is a comparative newcomer; Paricutín erupted in 1943 in Michoacán, about 250 miles southwest of Mexico City, and created a cone in what had once been a cornfield that was as flat as a tortilla. At the end of the first week the smoldering mass had reached 450 feet in height; at the end of two months it had reached 1,000 feet; and it rose to a total of 1,700 feet before finally lapsing into dormancy after nine years — by which time it had driven out the inhabitants of a village and smothered their houses.

An even more violent volcano, El Chichón, erupted in Chiapas in 1982. So enormous was the cloud of ash it sent aloft that it caused two days of darkness in nearby villages, and within a week it had turned the normally azure skies over far-off Hawaii a milky white.

The topography and the prevailing winds combine to give Mexico the most erratic of rainfalls. At least 70 percent of the country is classified as semiarid. Average annual rainfall varies widely, from less than three inches in some portions of the northwest to more than 175 inches in the tropical south. Roughly 75 percent of all rainfall occurs during the summer and autumn, and 65 percent of that amount is lost through evaporation, as well as through the regular transpiration of plants. According to one estimate, half of Mexico's land is dry throughout the year and another 37 percent suffers from seasonal droughts. Consequently, agriculture has presented a challenge throughout history.

Nevertheless, where the mountains divide to form broad basins and valleys, people have settled since prehistoric times. The valleys of Mexico, Morelos, Aguascalientes, Guanajuato, Jalisco, Puebla and Toluca have invited the heaviest concentrations of settlers; today they contain nearly 40 percent of the nation's cropland and are home to more than half of its population and the locus of five of Mexico's 10 largest cities, including the capital.

Here and there in the mountainous areas are pockets of pure-blooded Indians. They still use words that are not understood from one village to the next, and they honor ancient gods along with the Christian saints introduced by determined Spanish missionaries. Until recent times these far-flung settlements were connected (if at all) only by footpaths. The isolation afforded by the rugged terrain protected them from many other European traditions and made it possible for the villagers to continue the practices of Mexico's great ancient civilizations. These people provide a living link to the stone ruins of temples and holy

A burro and its rider cross the sand dunes of the wind-eroded tablelands of Coahuila in northern Mexico. This bleak state contains scarcely 4 percent of Mexico's population.

Makeshift housing dots the agricultural valley of Santiago in Central Mexico. Agrarian reform has fallen short of the revolutionary ideal of land for all, and as late as 1985 more than half of the rural population was living in one-room shacks.

places that are visible from the air.

Altogether, Mexico has something like 10,000 archeological sites. Only a few have been restored, but among them — Monte Albán, Teotihuacán, Palenque, Tula, Mitla, Chichén Itzá and Uxmal — are the nation's greatest cultural monuments. It is from these that archeologists have managed to piece together the history of the ancient peoples who lived and worshipped there. The Aztecs, who ruled much of Mexico when Spanish explorers arrived in the 16th century, were the last great people in a civilization that had begun 1,200 years before Christ. The achievements of these peoples — evident in art and in science and mathematics — are symbols of Mexican national pride, which withstood attack first by Spanish colonials and later by 19th-century Mexicans who were trying to modernize the nation.

The geological activity that formed the topography and influenced human settlement also pushed up deposits of silver, copper, gold, lead, iron, sulfur, cadmium, manganese, mercury, tungsten — more than 40 minerals that are vital to modern technology. And the lowlands along the Gulf Coast underwent periodic inundations by the sea, during which rich deposits of animal and vegetable matter were laid down. These metamorphosed eventually into fossil fuels. In 1984 Mexico was the world's fourth-largest producer of petroleum, and with 72 billion barrels, it was second only to Saudi Arabia in proven reserves.

The abundance of oil, together with all those minerals, and the country's expansion into such industries as steel, electric energy and automobiles, has enabled Mexico to build one of the fastest-growing manufacturing econo-

mies in the developing world; during the last three years of the 1970s, until the worldwide recession slowed the pace at the start of the 1980s, industrial production surged ahead by an average of 8.1 percent a year.

For all that, Mexico remains a poor nation. According to one estimate made in 1981, perhaps 5 percent of the nation's citizens live in luxury; 20 to 30 percent can be described as middle class; and more than 60 percent are poor, many of them existing at subsistence level. In the words of Mexican sociologist Pablo González Casanova, "There is an immense number of Mexicans who have nothing of nothing." Many of these dwell in the hundreds of slums, called *ciudades perdidas* (lost cities), in and around Mexico City — and in the thousands more that have cropped up in the countryside, where

The spires and façade of a church half-buried in lava are all that remain of the village of San Juan Parangaricutiro, 250 miles southwest of Mexico City. A volcanic cone sprang up in a nearby cornfield in 1943 and smothered the town with its eruptions.

more than half of the population inhabits one-room shacks that are without water or sanitation.

Close to 40 percent of the Mexican workers are still engaged in agriculture. The arrangements by which they farm have evolved by a tortuous path from ancient Indian customs — and have been accompanied by terrible growing pains with the emergence of the modern Mexican state.

Pre-Hispanic Indians farmed collectively; they lived in villages, tilling land outside the settlements where they resided and sharing their crops. Although during the time of Aztec rule they were required to pay some of their yield in tribute to the emperor and occasionally a further share to the nobles who fought on their behalf, the Indians nevertheless retained a certain measure of independence and regarded themselves as free. The Spaniards ap-

propriated the Indians' land, and they impressed those who lived on it.

As time passed, Spanish colonists and their descendants grew wealthy from the fruits of their enormous holdings. By 1910, according to a government census, most of the nation's land was divided among 8,245 private haciendas, or estates.

Resentment over such an egregious imbalance eventually erupted in the Mexican revolution, which was to overturn the entire social order by the time it ended in 1920. While the fighting still raged, the revolutionaries drafted a new constitution in 1917 that gave top priority to agrarian reform. The constitution established the government's sovereignty over the land, stating: "The nation shall at all times have the right to impose on private property such limitations as the public interest may demand." Later laws placed limits on the size of private lands, and established the right of groups of poor peasants to band together to claim unused land on which to form *ejidos,* or communal holdings: The formulas for *ejido* size were based on the number of members, the quality of the land and the products to be raised.

The government would first seize the land, paying the owner either in cash or, more typically, in government bonds; the price established was equivalent to the tax assessment of the property. Each *ejido,* administered by the peasant group, would then be parceled out to individual members or would be farmed communally. Every poor Mexican who was able to prove that he was engaged in agriculture was — and remains today — eligible for a parcel of land on which to raise food to feed his family.

Implementing the constitution was to be a slow and painful process, and nearly two decades passed before much was done about it. The undertaking began in earnest, however, in the middle 1930s, with the administration of General Lázaro Cárdenas, a man who endeared himself to his countrymen by the personal touch he brought to his office. He instituted the practice — now a well-established ritual — of periodic presidential tours through the countryside, attended by flag-waving crowds and speechmaking. He ordered wells to be dug and promised land to the peasants who crowded around him in every village.

Cárdenas kept his promise. Land redistribution became the centerpiece of his regime, and by the time he left office in 1940 after a six-year term, his government had made 50 million acres of land available in one way or another to more than two million peasants.

HARVEST FROM THE WATERS

One of Mexico's great — largely unused — resources is fish. With its 6,000 miles of coastline, the country could tap more than 100 species of fish and shellfish to feed the population and earn export income. Yet most fishing is done primitively, as seen in these pictures of Zapotec Indian fisherfolk. The men travel half an hour by train, from their town of Juchitán, on the Gulf of Tehuantepec, then walk five miles to their fishing grounds on the shallow Laguna Superior. There they wade out perhaps a mile to cast their nets.

At night they return with their catch to the village. The women sell the fish the next day in the marketplace; leftover fish is dried and smoked to be sold later.

Wading out in a lagoon, fishermen cast their nets. They wear baskets on their hips to hold their catch and equipment.

Gutted fish are spread out to dry in the sun on an improvised rack — an old bedspring.

24

The women clean the fish as pigs scavenge at their feet for scraps.

1

The expropriation of private land-holdings was radical, but the basic concept of the *ejido* — despite its Spanish name — was as old as Mexico. A peasant could hold and work the particular *ejido* that was provided him by the government — just as an ancient Indian had worked a particular parcel that was considered to be the property of his people at large. In the modern version the peasant could for all practical purposes pass his *ejido* on to a single heir, but he could not divide it among several children and he could not sell it. If he did not use it as farmland, his parcel was forfeited, to be given away to someone else.

As the plan took effect, wells, plows, hoes and other farm implements already on the land of the haciendas became the property of all, and the new landowners, the peasants, shared them. Also collectively, the peasants purchased fertilizers, insecticides and seeds. To enable the peasants to buy what they needed for agriculture, the Cárdenas government established the National Ejidal Credit Bank. To teach the people how to use their new land, it sent engineers and agronomists out through the countryside.

All things considered, the program got off to an encouraging start. The most dramatic and successful example of the expropriations Cárdenas instituted took place in the Laguna region in north-central Mexico. There the government seized more than a million acres of already efficiently organized and modernized cotton plantations from the *hacendados*, the owners, and turned them over to 38,000 peasant families. This was done in just 40 days, too fast for the *hacendados* to muster much opposition.

Once they received title to the land, the peasants joined in scores of cooperatives and eventually learned to operate the plantations as effectively as the landlords had done. During the first three years of the *ejido* program, in one part of the Laguna region, as peasants began to realize profits from their farming, their purchasing power increased more than 400 percent.

For the country as a whole, agricultural production for the three-year period ending in 1941 was higher than it had been in more than 30 years, since before the revolution. Although the pace of distribution slowed as subsequent presidents devoted more attention to other sectors of the economy — developing mineral resources and embarking on industrialization — the total land given to peasants by 1980 equaled about 150 million acres.

Gone forever was the peonage that prevailed at the turn of the century. For the first time, Mexico's peasants had a real stake in the economy of their nation as a whole, and expectations of improving their lot.

Inevitably, not all the high hopes could be met. A burgeoning population (with a phenomenal growth rate of more than 3 percent per year throughout the 1950s, 1960s, 1970s and early 1980s) has combined with a sluggish bureaucracy to burden the *ejido* program with grave problems. *Ejidos* by law cannot be divided, and a peasant father is apt to leave five or six offspring who cannot inherit his land and who therefore must apply to the government for parcels of their own.

At the start of the 1980s there were 3.5 million peasants legally entitled to claim land, but no efficient way of distributing what land was available. The Secretariat of Agrarian Reform had a backlog of petitions for new *ejidos* numbering nearly 200,000. "I've beaten a trail to Mexico City — I've gone to the Secretariat many times," Alfredo Figueroa, who represented 556 families petitioning for land in Oaxaca, told an American reporter. "Always the offices are crowded with people like me who have a lot of documents and hardly a shred of hope."

Added to this are other problems that the government has not solved. From the beginning, many of the big landowners protected their holdings from expropriation by dividing them into parcels smaller than the legal limit on private lands and distributing the plots to family members; they then continued to farm them as before. Being just as likely as peasants to have large families, the *hacendados* thus had no difficulty retaining control of vast tracts. In the state of Sinaloa, a landholder by the name of Alejandro Canelos controls a 1,700-acre farm that is divided among seven family members. "We are within the law," he declared to an American journalist. "You can't tell the difference between the properties, but on paper they are separate."

More spectacularly, a Jalisco landholder owns about 12,500 acres of ranchland, on which he grazes as many as 2,000 head of cattle. He and 63 other landowners held 83 percent of a 425-square-mile area surveyed in 1978.

Many *hacendados* who did comply strictly with the law made it work to their own advantage, using their compensation from the government to set themselves up as entrepreneurs — selling seed, fertilizers, insecticides, feed and farm equipment to the peasants. In some instances, that arrangement also worked to the peasants' advantage; it meant that they had the wherewithal of farming ready to hand.

Making do with the old ways, a Mexican farmer uses an ox-drawn cart to trundle a load of straw down a road by Lake Patzcuaro in Michoacán. Here villagers still plant corn, beans and squash by hand, and sell their meager crops at market on Sundays.

For many peasants, however, the prospects remain grim. Although in theory holders of *ejidos* can get credit from the government-sponsored Ejidal Credit Bank, in practice they are often unable to do so because the great demand outstrips the available funds. And they cannot apply to other banks because by law they cannot use *ejido* land as collateral. For a seed loan they may have to pay a usurious 100 percent interest to some *hacendado*-turned-agribusinessman, or as much as 50 percent to a loan shark who then gets the right to buy their crops at whatever price he sets. In desperation, many *ejidatarios* rent their plots to agribusinesses and then go to work as hired hands on their own land.

The existence of such inequities has given the government pause. It remains both constitutionally and emotionally committed to the ideal of land for all. But large farms are generally considered to be more efficient and more profitable than the *ejidos*. This is because the well-to-do farmers can buy the latest in equipment and fertilizers, and plenty of both. And they can afford to specialize in certain high-profit products — tomatoes, cucumbers, strawberries, coffee and pearl onions — which bring big prices in the export market and valuable foreign exchange for the government.

That in itself might not be controversial. But the fact is that Mexico is not raising sufficient food to feed itself. Food imports for the early 1980s averaged 12 million tons annually. Among these was corn, the very foodstuff that supplied and made possible Mexico's earliest civilization, and the one on which it is dependent even today. Hence the government faces a dilemma. Should it encourage the farming of crops for export (which bring in much-needed cash) or instead press the farmers to produce enough food to feed their fellow Mexicans?

A further dilemma is posed by the farming operations themselves. Big operations make higher productivity possible. Should the government therefore help the rich achieve the higher productivity that a developing nation needs? Or should it continue to honor the goals of the constitution by finding land for everyone who wants it?

"People thought all their troubles would be solved if they just had three acres and a cow," says Paul LaMartine Yates, a British agricultural economist versed in Mexican affairs. But of the three million families who had acquired *ejidal* parcels by the 1980s, only about 400,000, according to one estimate, have substantially improved their standard of living.

The typical Mexican peasant farms his *ejido* with the help of household labor only; one adult with a team of horses and a child helper can cultivate at best four hectares, about 10 acres, which will yield just enough to feed his own family. The plow the peasant farmer uses is much like the wooden-tipped Mediterranean plows brought by the Spanish conquistadors, the only improvement being steel tips that can displace small stones without being worn down. The crops are even older — the ancient Indians' hallowed beans, squash and, above all, corn.

No matter what crops are grown, the daily routine is much the same from one farm to another. The men of most farming families rise at daybreak, and after a breakfast of beans and tortillas and sweet black coffee, they set out for the fields. Some return home at midday

for their main meal; most pause in the fields to consume a meal brought to them by the women. In either case, the meal is likely to be beans and tortillas again, sometimes dressed up with meat, onions, tomatoes, garlic and chilis. When they return home in the evening they snack — perhaps on corn gruel, often on tortillas again.

The job of preparing the tortillas falls to the farmwife. There are some women now who buy machine-made tortillas in a village store and heat them before serving, but many a wife makes her own in the traditional way. She starts in the evening, dissolving a little lime in water and adding dried corn. In the warmth of the kitchen the kernels swell during the night. At five in the morning she takes the soaked corn out to the village mill, where it is crushed into a dough. Back at home, she slaps small lumps of this dough into thin rounds, which she cooks over the fire on a pottery griddle. In an hour's time she can make 60 or 70, one day's supply for a family of five.

The corn from which the tortillas are made has, from prehistoric times to the present, been both a blessing and an inhibiting factor in Mexico's development. It can be considered a blessing because the cultivation of corn enabled the prehistoric Indians to settle down and develop a civilization, but at the same time it has inhibited too many Mexicans from trying to raise anything else. The late anthropologist Alfredo Barrera Vázquez once set out from the Yucatán city of Mérida to visit a newly discovered archeological zone in the nearby state of Campeche. He stopped at a farm and asked the woman of the house if she could prepare a meal, saying he would gladly pay her.

"I am sorry, señor," the woman re-

Fieldworkers harvest the *ágave tequilero*, whose fleshy rootstock will be cooked, ground, fermented and distilled to yield tequila, the nation's fiery-tasting and potent beverage. The plant is a succulent with broad leaves that retain moisture.

1

sponded to him, "but we have no food."

"But," said the anthropologist, "you have a cow — you must have milk and butter, perhaps cheese. You have chickens — there must be eggs. And I can see beans growing in your garden."

"That is true," said the woman, "but we have no real food. A *bicho* [insect] and the *sequía* [drought] killed our corn crop and we are starving."

In the observation of the agricultural economist Edmundo Flores, corn is for Mexicans "a basic need, a dietary obsession and a nightmare for the minister of agriculture." Because their diet depends too much on corn and because they do not grow enough of it, a scant 18 percent of the population — according to the standards of the National Program for Nutrition — are considered to be well nourished.

In Oaxaca, a scientist using measurements of bone structure compared the bodies of present-day Oaxacans with skeletons in ancient graves. He concluded that today's people are no better nourished than their ancestors of 1,000 years ago. Another study, conducted in 1972, found that 33 percent of the Mexican population seldom had enough milk to drink, and 6 percent barely knew what milk was.

Mexican peasants today are divided between those who have resigned themselves to their lot and those who are seeking escape. In Coahuila, not far from the Rio Grande (called Río Bravo in Mexico), Urbano Rosales, a wiry man of middle age, has lived for 25 years by picking from the desert the edible weed *lechuguilla,* a thistly variety of wild lettuce. He works 14 hours a day to earn enough for a seldom-changing diet of tortillas and beans. When a political scientist asked Urbano's wife, Ofelia, who had borne him 10 children, why he did

Chilis, cheese and tomatoes garnish a tasty tortilla.

When the Spaniards arrived in Mexico, they found a whole new world of food to enjoy. But there were also items too bizarre for them to relish — dog, newt with yellow chili, winged ants, corn smut, waterfly eggs, and dried algae, which Aztec warriors carried on campaigns as a convenient, protein-rich ration. And though the Spaniards loved the Indians' chocolate, they were not particularly fond of the Aztec habit of flavoring hot cocoa with hot chilis.

Fortunately, the foods the Spaniards did like quickly caught on in other countries. Among these were turkey and two of today's staples — beans and corn.

Corn's worldwide acceptance among the poor was a mixed blessing. Those who depended almost totally on corn for food developed pellagra, and thousands died. Not until this century, however, did scientists discover the link between corn and the disease: The body is unable to digest corn's niacin. But then why had the Indians who had eaten corn-meal tortillas three times a day — and often little else — not gotten the disease? The solution to the mystery lay in the method of preparation they used. To soften their dried corn, they soaked it in slaked lime and water. The lime rendered the niacin digestible, thus enabling this important B vitamin to be absorbed and utilized by the body.

not look for easier and more productive work elsewhere, she replied, "The land sticks to his feet." The man himself — his inertia compounded by optimism — had a more poignant answer. "You wait and see," he said; "this year it will rain and we will no longer be poor."

Such optimism is unrealistic, but widespread. "From the highways you can see groups of peasants in the open fields kneeling around statues of the Virgin, desperately praying for rain," the governor of the small state of Tlaxcala, east of Mexico City, told a foreign reporter. "It did not rain last year nor this year either. If it does not rain by mid-June the crops are lost because corn planted after that is killed by the autumn frosts before it ripens. Peasants either plant corn or move to the city."

Cynical Mexicans use an old expression, *"Sal si puedes"* — "Get out if you can" — in the spirit of a dare. In increasing numbers, Mexicans are doing just that. Some make their way across the border to the United States, where higher wages and standards of living act as an economic suction pump. "You never make the money here that you make in the United States," a peasant named José López told a reporter in 1979. In that year the minimum wage in Tijuana was $7.13 a day, while in California, just across the border, it was $23.20 a day.

With higher wages go creature comforts that are hard to come by in rural Mexico. "In Los Angeles I had a nice car for $940," a long-haired young Mexican who shuttled illegally between the American city and his village told an American journalist. "Here having any car is impossible. I have to go everywhere by bus or walk. There I had heat and air conditioning and a telephone. Our village has one phone, in the

schoolhouse, but it's been out of order for three or four years."

Immigration quotas limit to 20,000 the number of Mexicans who can cross the border legally each year. No one knows how many slip across illegally, but according to the U.S. Bureau of the Census, an estimated 3.5 to 6 million Mexicans are living in the United States without proper documents. Some, who can scrape up the $400 fee, contract with a "coyote" to get them into the U.S.; they travel in covered trucks,

cooped up like chickens, for which reason they are known as *pollos*. Others, lacking the money to pay a coyote, attempt to cross at remote spots. They are frequently caught by border police, who turn them back — but they keep on trying, and some do succeed after three or four attempts.

Not all migrants head across the border. Some go to the cities of Coatzacoalcos and Villahermosa on the Gulf Coast, where Pemex — Petróleos Mexicanos, the Mexican oil industry — pro-

vides employment clearing oil fields, driving trucks and serving as guards. Others go to Ciudad Juárez, Nogales, Nuevo Laredo and Tijuana, border towns where foreign-owned industries have set up factories to take advantage of the low labor rates. Still others go to such coastal resorts as Acapulco and Cancún; in the early 1980s tourism employed 650,000 Mexicans.

But the main magnet is their own capital, Mexico City. In the decade of the 1970s some six million males between the ages of 15 and 30 arrived there — at an average rate of 1,370 a day. A few find employment as unskilled laborers, digging, shoveling, carrying building materials. But uncounted numbers swell the ranks of the unemployed. That fact has helped give the municipal as well as the federal government problems that are well-nigh insoluble. "If we become careless," President Miguel de la Madrid said in 1983, "Mexico City can become uninhabitable." ☐

Cone-shaped silos stand in a row outside Puebla, 65 miles southeast of Mexico City. Such silos are maintained nationwide by the government, which aids farmers by buying and storing their grain until it is bought by merchants and big-city mills.

A MEXICAN SUCCESS STORY

In the sere highlands of Querétaro, about 115 miles northwest of Mexico City, lies an exemplary ranch. Here, 28-year-old Jorge Roiz, the second-oldest of nine children, manages on behalf of his father a 1,500-head dairy herd. In the 10 years that he has been in charge, he has increased milk production to more than 5,000 gallons a day, making the ranch one of the 10 top producers in the country. And as a sideline, he raises bulls for the ring. To oversee the work of the ranch, Jorge is constantly in motion, traveling in his truck across the land and making radio contact with his 300 workers. Because of the ranch's success, he has the financial resources to keep up with the latest developments in animal husbandry — technology unavailable to most smaller farmers.

Modern techniques of farming have not encroached on certain Mexican traditions, however. Jorge's wife, Luz María Amieva de Roiz, stays home to raise their three-year-old son, Jorgito; and her father, another wealthy rancher, lives nearby with her mother, so the extended family maintains intimate ties.

With son Jorgito in his arms, wife Luz at his side and a German shepherd at his feet, rancher Jorge Roiz relaxes in front of his stone house.

Jorge inspects his herd. Corrals prevent the cows from grazing at will, and on machine-mixed grain they yield 5,285 gallons of milk daily.

Jorge takes notes as neighboring small landholders bring him their farming problems.

Jorge assists a ranch hand at the breech birth of a calf.

The cow nuzzles her newborn calf.

Jorge watches an aspiring matador
test a heifer for temperament. If she
proves aggressive enough, she will
be separated from the milk cows and
used to breed toros for the bull ring.

José Calzada, an 18-year-old *novillero* — apprentice matador — flashes his red cape. Aspiring bullfighters visit the ranch regularly; in testing the heifers for Jorge Roiz they get practice.

José waves the cape, lures the heifer forward and deftly eludes her charge. At the conclusion of the exercise the young bullfighter will evaluate the heifer's reactions for Jorge.

37

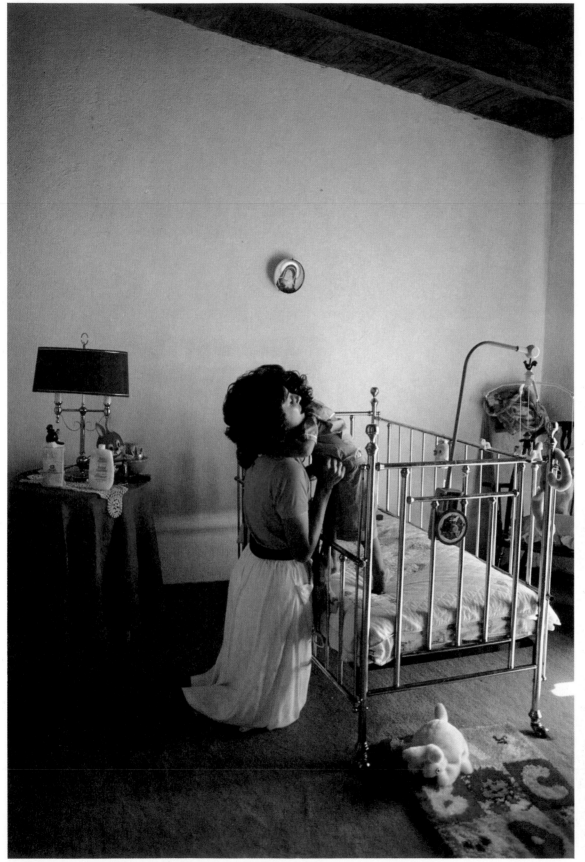

Mother and son hug as Luz gets Jorgito up from an afternoon nap.

Luz washes Jorgito's hair in a
custom-built shower stall large enough
for his many bath toys.

In a living room filled with antiques
and modern furniture, Jorgito plays in
a sneaker-shaped kiddy car.

Luz's father, Remigio Amieva Noriega, shows his grandson Jorgito two of the 100 prize race horses he breeds at his own ranch.

Seated with her mother and father, her brother and a guest, Luz and Jorge *(center)* enjoy a hearty breakfast at her parents' house. Living close by, the families frequently share meals.

Rising majestically behind Mexico City on a relatively smogless day is the snow-capped volcano of Popocatépetl (Smoking Mountain), at 17,887 feet one of the tallest peaks in Mexico. The sprawling metropolis is the world's fastest growing, with 18 million people in an area of 586 square miles.

A CITY ON THE BRINK OF HELL

An English journalist once wrote that "if every day could be Sunday, Mexico City would qualify as one of the most enchanting cities on earth." On that day of leisure, he found, the people cast aside their weekly cares and become a "new race of relaxed and smiling country folk" intent on quiet family picnics in the city's beautiful 1,000-acre Chapultepec Park or on long sessions of good-natured bargaining at colorful outdoor flea markets. Some of the normally frenetic downtown areas take on the air of a huge fiesta with vendors hawking tacos and tortillas while mariachi bands (there are about 6,000 of these in the city) fill the air with music.

Mexico City at its best is one of the world's most entrancing metropolises. It is the oldest major city in the New World and can boast of having had the first Christian church, the first library, the first hospital and the first university in the Americas. Many ancient buildings survive, some dating back almost to the Spanish conquest of 1521, along with relics of the Aztecs who had made the place their capital two centuries before that time.

The city remains not only Mexico's political capital, but also its artistic, cultural and intellectual center. Here are most of Mexico's book-publishing firms and the country's film industry. The city's presses produce 20 daily papers and at least 235 periodicals of every political and artistic persuasion. Its television studios pour out shows that are al-most exhausting in their variety and inventiveness. Dozens of galleries selling the works of Mexico's contemporary painters and sculptors attest to the citizens' enthusiasm for art.

The people themselves are vivid and colorful, a handsome mixture of Mexico's Indian and Spanish heritages. Here is a profile as noble as those incised on Aztec or Toltec pyramids and temples. There is a delicate, high-cheekboned face straight from a painting by El Greco or Velázquez. Skin tones range from Spanish pale to deep Indian brown. Old faces are weathered to a monumental dignity; demure and dark-eyed children look more angelic than seems humanly possible.

These are people who love a good time and who relax as energetically as they work, packing the world's largest bull ring, the 60,000-seat Plaza de Mexico, as well as a score of other stadiums to become vocal participants in soccer matches, bullfights, *jai alai* games, horse races, Mexican-style rodeos and U.S.-style *beisbol*. They patronize hundreds of restaurants that offer some of the world's best beer and most interesting food, ranging from refried beans to less-well-known viands such as *huitlacoche,* a fungus that grows on corn, and dishes spiced with any of 140 varieties of chili peppers.

The city boasts dozens of fine modern buildings and a pair of great boulevards that rival those of Paris or Madrid. The Avenida de los Insurgentes, whose name commemorates the patriots who threw off Spanish rule during Mexico's struggle for independence in the early part of the 19th century, is a grand 14 miles long. The Paseo de la Reforma, named for the liberal reforms enacted in the late 19th century, is wider than any of the Parisian boulevards after which it was modeled, and sections of it are lined with shops of Continental elegance. The handsome homes of well-to-do residents grace such leafy enclaves as Las Lomas (the hills) de Chapultepec, while the San Angel area remains a reserve of lovely Spanish colonial mansions.

Even the climate is benign. Although Mexico City lies well within the tropics, its 7,350-foot elevation keeps the capital from being oppressively hot or humid. The annual mean temperature is 65° F., and it varies little between winter and summer.

Mexico City is most remarkable today, however, not for its age, beauty, climate or people, but for its size. Greater Mexico City — the 172-square-mile Federal District and its burgeoning outskirts — has become the fastest-growing city on earth and, with the exception of Greater Tokyo, the largest. By the mid-1980s the Mexico City metropolitan area had 17.5 million people versus Tokyo's 23 million. If Mexico City continues to grow as swiftly as it has grown since the 1970s, it will be home to an estimated 32 million human beings by the year 2000, more than the projected populations of Paris, London and Moscow combined.

It is the city's huge and vibrant population that makes Sundays seem such special, smiling days. The rest of the week for a majority of the inhabitants brings a gut-wrenching struggle with grid-locked traffic, jammed subways

High atop her column, Winged Victory looks down on the Paseo de la Reforma. She symbolizes freedom from Spanish rule, obtained during the 1810-1821 War of Independence. Dedicated in 1910, the monument was toppled in the 1957 earthquake and rebuilt; it withstood the 1985 quake.

and jostling pedestrian mobs. Should the city grow as predicted, these nightmarish conditions can only get worse. Mexico City sits in a bowl hemmed in by mountains and, although the entire metropolitan area covers a huge 586 square miles, it cannot expand outward very much more.

Other factors contribute to the city's problems. Almost two thirds of the inhabitants are poor, many desperately so, and the slum areas they live in are so extensive that Mexico City ranks first in the world in acreage given over to shantytowns. The city can also claim another dubious distinction: the world's worst air pollution. It is, in short, a city in crisis, a crisis of the sort that many great cities may face in the last years of the 20th century.

Sociologists, environmentalists and urban planners all over the world are attentively watching Mexico City to see if it can survive its problems, and to see if the steps it takes to cope are effective or not. In the meantime, Mexico City, despite its many charms and attractions, will be a difficult place to live for most of its citizens. "It is not that we have been expelled from paradise," author Fernando Benitez has said. "Rather, we have expelled paradise itself."

Mexico City's crowding can be traced back partly to the unsettling events of history. During the revolution of 1910-1920, about 1.2 million farmfolk fled from the war-torn countryside to seek the comparative safety of the cities, and about a third of them ended up in the capital. A further influx occurred when, after the revolution, the government broke up the large estates that had dominated the agricultural scene and gave farmsteads to the landless *campesinos*. Regrettably, there was not enough land to go around, and many of the peons without farms migrated to the cities. So did other *campesinos* who, released from virtual serfdom on the haciendas, were glad to throw down their hoes and look for other work. Since that time the flow has continued, rising to a flood in recent decades.

Aside from all its other attractions, Mexico City has been the place with the most and best jobs. The federal government alone employs about 1.5 million people, and the city is the focus of Mexican industry. In some ways this development has made sense despite the city's distance, about 200 miles, from the water transport offered by Mexico's coasts, the Pacific to the west and the Gulf of Mexico to the east. When industrialization began in the 1940s, the city was already the hub of the nation's road and rail network. It was also the banking center; today seven of every 10 banking transactions in Mexico take place there. And it was where both wealth and people were concentrated, making it Mexico's largest consumer market.

The factories that sprang up created jobs, and the prospect of jobs drew more and more *campesinos* to the city. This burgeoning labor pool in turn attracted more factories. One jobs-minded national administration after another encouraged the proliferation of smoke-belching mills by granting entrepreneurs exceptions from Mexico's otherwise strict antipollution laws. By the 1980s more than 50 percent of all the country's industries were concentrated in Mexico City.

The trouble has been that even in prosperous times there have never been enough jobs to employ all the people lured to the city by the promise of factory work. This has not stopped the headlong emigration from the villages,

The floodlit Plaza of the Three Cultures encapsulates Mexico's history in the ruin of the Aztec pyramid of Tlatelolco, the façade of the colonial church of Santiago and the modern buildings of Mexico City. It was in this area that the last battle between the Spaniards and the Aztecs was fought.

however. Even when jobs have proved illusory, many *campesinos* have preferred to eke out a living in the city's slums rather than remain in the country, performing the backbreaking labor necessary to coax sparse crops from the stony and often drought-plagued soil.

Some of Mexico City's overcrowding is a direct result of the nation's high birth rate and a lowered death rate. But the main reason for the city's explosive growth has been the influx of millions of peasants escaping from rural areas all over the nation.

With the population running far ahead of the number of jobs, unemployment has climbed dizzily and the growth of slum areas has gotten out of control. By recent estimates, one third of the city's work force is unemployed or underemployed. And the wages earned even by those with steady jobs in industry are often desperately low. A beginning production-line worker in the typical Mexico City factory takes home 680 pesos a day. Like their jobless brethren, these workers cannot afford the inflated rents charged in the newer and better apartment developments. They, too, must live in the endlessly proliferating slums.

The capital's slums are a fascinating study in themselves and have attracted social anthropologists from all over the world. They seem to grow and mutate with a life of their own. There are approximately 500 slums large and small fringing the city's perimeter and a few more scattered through the center. Some of those on the outskirts are so long-established and comparatively livable that they scarcely deserve to be called slums. All of them are nevertheless known by the sinister name *ciudades perdidas,* or "lost cities." And all are tributes to the amount of hardship the

2

Mexican people can endure, and to their ingenuity as well.

The largest and one of the oldest of the blue-collar areas on the edge of the Federal District is Ciudad Nezahual-cóyotl, City of the Hungry Coyote. Neza, as it is known, boasted a population of about three million in the early 1980s, making it the world's largest slum. Twenty square miles in area, it is situated in the dry bed of what was once part of a salt lake. When the wind is blowing, the dust stings the eyes and clogs the throat.

The older sections of Neza have been there long enough to have acquired paved main streets — although side streets of rutted dirt are still common — and municipal services such as water mains and electricity. In fact, the residents, in a remarkable show of civic unity, refused to make any mortgage payments on the land, originally bought from unscrupulous developers, until such services were provided. But most of the dwellings remain concrete-block and corrugated-iron shanties at best, and at worst lean-tos of scrap lumber and jerry cans pounded flat. Garbage heaps attended by clouds of flies still make it necessary for motorists who are driving through to close the windows of their automobiles.

The slums keep growing. Some are extensions of existing ones; Neza has its own suburban areas. Others are born overnight when homeless families suddenly occupy a patch of vacant land. Indeed, so swiftly do these people seem to descend on such areas to erect their shanties of cardboard, tarpaper, wood and whatever else comes to hand that they have been nicknamed *paracaidistas,* or "parachutists."

The new arrivals are often cheated of their meager funds by swindlers who claim to own the land on which the squatters have built their flimsy dwellings. Knowing no better, they pay rent to the swindlers. And what happens more often is that the squatters are forced to pay protection money to self-appointed slum bosses or to the police.

Despite such payments, any new arrivals until recently stood a good chance of being run off by the authorities. Nowadays the government is more likely to let them stay, even eventually granting them title to the land they occupy. In the long run, as it has at Neza, the government will send bulldozers to grade the streets between the shacks and will bring in water mains and electricity. Until that time, the squatters employ their ingenuity, illegally tapping the nearest power line with their own wires and siphoning water from a handy main if there is one. After that, new arrivals are likely to add to their flimsy shelters only portable improvements such as television sets. Investing in better houses is something that can wait for the day when the government has ratified their claim on the land.

By all odds the most noxious of the city's slums are those that are located literally on top of a dozen or so municipal garbage dumps. The denizens of the dumps survive by scavenging amid the refuse for anything — paper, glass or metal, perhaps broken household items — that can be recycled or fixed. Living in a horrid stench that they no longer even notice, the dump dwellers also tend small flocks of pigs and goats, which root for sustenance side by side with their owners.

The stoic endurance of the scavengers is matched by the ingenuity and hard work of the inhabitants of what is probably Mexico City's most comfortable squatter town, a community known by the name of Belén de las Flores, or Bethlehem of the Flowers. Here, on a terraced hillside not far from Chapultepec Park, the inhabitants have hollowed out snug caves and planted small garden plots by their doorways. Running past the gardens along the terraces are well-swept dirt streets punctuated by utility poles.

Whether cave dwellers or citizens of the dumps, the slumfolk count themselves fortunate to be in Mexico City. "We thank God for letting us live here," a taxi driver named Esteban Mendez Gonzales recently said, nodding toward the noisome slum called Devil's Curve where he, his wife and their six children live in a wood-and-tarpaper shack amid 1,500 other *paracaidistas.* Another squatter, when he was asked why he and his family had come to a similar shantytown, replied forthrightly, "It was plain ignorance. We came because we thought it would be heaven here. But it's not, is it?" He went on to explain why, despite all the difficulties, he did not intend to go back home. "In Oaxaca, I went to school but I didn't learn to read or write, really. But here, if my children go to school and if they wear better clothes, well, maybe it will be better for them."

The hope that life will be better for their children, if not for themselves, buoys many *paracaidistas.* Mexico City's public schools tend to be better than those in most provincial cities, and they are infinitely superior to rural schools, which are poorly funded and have small teaching staffs. Mexico City schools, with their larger budgets, can afford more teachers and attract many of the nation's best. After finishing the compulsory first six years, many students go on to high school. In the six elementary-school years the students

A HARD, PROUD LIFE IN A TEEMING SLUM

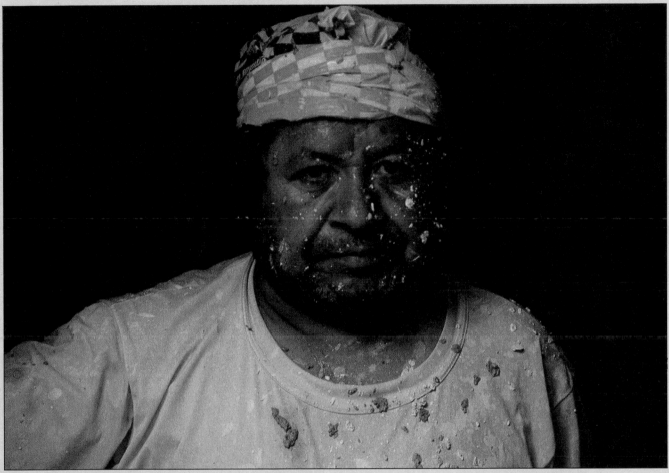

His face splattered with plaster, mason Juan Mijangos Muñoz takes a moment's rest during his work at a construction site.

Home for Juan Mijangos Muñoz is a jerry-built house on a garbage-strewn street in Nezahualcóyotl, a slum of three million just outside Mexico City. But it is a house to be proud of. Mijangos lives there happily with his wife Agripina, their four boys, his mother, his wife's parents and several nonrelatives to whom he rents rooms.

Mijangos, who is typical of Mexico's urban poor, came to Mexico City from the country in 1948, when he was only nine, to live with an aunt and to find a job. He had one year of schooling and hired himself out as a mason's assistant.

After several years of hard work, he had enough money saved to buy some camera equipment and a donkey. He then began making a living going from one residential area to another, taking pictures of children astride the animal. But when the capital's ever-increasing traffic congestion became unbearable (the donkey finally refused to budge and had to be carted off in a truck), Mijangos abandoned photography and went back to being a mason.

By that time he had purchased a small lot in "Neza," the dusty site of a dried-up lake, whose bed was

so saturated with salts that most plants refused to grow on it. The community lacked public services of any kind — no water, electricity or garbage collection — but people flocked to it all the same, drawn by the cheapness of the land.

Here Mijangos built himself a one-room house, married and settled down. Time and money permitting, he has been adding to his house ever since, often with his wife's assistance. It is three stories tall and still growing, and Neza — which has yet to be incorporated into the capital — ranks now as the country's second largest city.

Agripina, Mijangos' wife, serves
stew to her husband and children while
the family television set flickers
above their heads. Following custom,
they use *tortillas* instead of
knives and forks, and scoop up or roll
up their food in them.

One of the boys makes the beds in the room that the immediate family uses for sleeping.

Mijangos climbs to the rooftop toilet and washing facilities; the family keeps its chickens on the roof, too.

Mijangos' mother lives in this room, which, in addition to her bed, contains the altar where she prays daily. Here she also cooks her own food.

Sitting in the doorway of the room that they occupy on the roof, Mijangos' mother- and father-in-law embroider tablecloths for the tourist trade. They came to Nezahualcóyotl when the husband needed medical treatment and then they stayed on, eking out a living from their stitchery.

Preparing her meal on a two-burner gas stove, Mijangos' mother waits for the pot to boil. Her daughter lives in the house next door, and with all the grandchildren around, she never lacks for company.

To celebrate a son's birthday,
Mijangos and family go off to a fair,
whose Ferris wheel can be seen in
the distance. Such outings are rare
because of the cost involved.

learn to read and write and are taught geography, mathematics, some biology and sociology, and the rudiments of Mexican history.

Whatever hopes Mexico City's *para-caidistas* may entertain for their children, life for many of these slum dwellers still remains difficult to the point of desperation. Those who are too elderly or too unskilled to find any work at all have a hand-to-mouth existence. Antonia Recindes, who spent more than 50 years of her life in a onetime country town named Tlanepaltla that has long since been swallowed up by the city, has survived in large measure on the meager sustenance still offered by her once-rural home. "As long as they don't increase the price of tortillas," she has said, "and as long as we can fill them with *nopales* [an edible cactus that grows nearby] or other wild vegetables or just anything, we'll get by."

Other unemployed residents of the *ciudades perdidas* make a little money doing a wide variety of odd jobs. Some work as part-time gardeners for the well-to-do in the high-walled estates off the Paseo de la Reforma, or as handymen in the affluent suburbs. Women also act as housemaids in these enclaves of the rich. Other unemployed men and women become sidewalk peddlers, selling fruits, nuts, homemade dolls or trinkets to passersby. Some of the men work as porters at the airport or as car washers. Some of the women beg or become prostitutes.

A number of skilled artisans gather every day outside the magnificent Metropolitan Cathedral in the downtown section of Mexico City, where they hold an informal job mart. These unemployed craftsmen wait patiently for someone to come by who needs their services. Until the economic crisis of the early 1980s brought runaway inflation and even more severe unemployment, many of them found work quite easily. "The crisis has changed everything," said one. "In previous years I used to come here at 8 in the morning and be whisked away to work. It has never been this difficult before."

Only one government-run welfare agency offers help to the unemployed. This is the Public Assistance Fund, which is financed by a small tax levied on lottery tickets sold by the government. The fund provides shelter and some food for the really desperate, but is still too small to come close to meeting the need.

This meager official effort is supplemented by several private agencies, some run by churches, some by public-spirited wives of government ministers. The largest is traditionally patronized by the country's president; it funds hospitals and nurseries and provides some assistance for the homeless. Mexico's social security system, with its medical benefits, unfortunately is of very little help to the slum dwellers. To qualify, a citizen must have had a job at some time, which is exactly what most *para-caidistas* cannot claim.

Some of the more fortunate immigrants to Mexico City — or more often their better-educated children — eventually manage to escape the slums and join at least the lower ranks of the middle class by finding full-time work as skilled artisans or as white-collar workers in government or industry. The middle class in Mexico City is now sizable and growing. It ranges from shopkeepers and office clerks at the bottom to professional people such as doctors and lawyers at the top. In general they share the difficulties and aspirations of the middle class everywhere in the world, but here the disparities in income and life style between bottom and top are much greater than in more developed economies.

For those at the bottom, the struggle to hang on can be almost as hard as it is for the poor. They must live in cramped quarters, perhaps shared with relatives, enjoy a minimum of consumer goods, rely on public transportation and limit their holiday excursions to public parks. They seldom go hungry and just as seldom dine out. Their finances are usually precarious; any setback can lead to disaster. "These are the guys I worry about," said a U.S. businessman in Mexico City, "the clerk in our office who has one suit and maybe two shirts and three kids and is hanging on by his fingernails."

With good luck some of these people make it to the comparative affluence of a small secondhand car, a two- or three-room apartment, domestic help and an occasional trip out of town. If they scrimp and save, they may be able to send their children to one of the city's excellent private academies, which offer their graduates the chance of advancement into the upper ranks of the middle class.

Many of these families bolster their upward efforts with two incomes. Women make up twice as much of the work force in Mexico City as elsewhere in the country — a revolutionary development for a Latin American nation. The older women tend to remain in "genteel" jobs such as shop assistant. The younger ones, usually more liberated and better educated, become secretaries in business offices or government bureaus. A very few make it into the professions.

A typical two-income middle-class family interviewed recently by an

53

2

Fresh from her first Communion, a girl in white lifts the hem of her gown as she climbs to her family's hut perched atop the garbage dump of Santa Fe in southwest Mexico City. Hundreds of people live here; inured to the stench, most earn a living scavenging for salable items.

American writer lived in a pleasant three-room apartment in Villa Kennedy, a huge housing complex named for the American president after his 1962 visit to Mexico. The husband worked in the government's Ministry of Housing, the wife as a grade-school teacher. Their two teen-age children were receiving good educations at one of the public secondary schools and had ambitions to go on to a university. All four members of the family were glad they had moved to Mexico City from a provincial city a decade before; the capital offered more opportunity, better salaries, better schools and a generally more exciting life.

Problems, nevertheless, intruded on this upwardly mobile, white-collar existence. Mexico City's high prices largely negated the higher salaries. The family's vacations were spent not traveling but relaxing in the nearby green oasis of Balbuena Park. Meals, though nourishing enough, often were built around tortillas and other inexpensive Mexican ingredients, and such equally cheap fare as ground beef mixed with a meat-stretching soybean-based product. This family, like many other white-collar people, found itself frequently frustrated by the red tape of a ubiquitous bureaucracy and worried by the steadily rising cost of shelter in the housing-short capital.

The members of the upper middle class — successful lawyers, doctors and other professionals, and the owners of the larger stores — live in attractive homes, enjoy more varied diets and can afford to send their children to private schools. Their evenings are often spent dining in some of Mexico City's many fine restaurants or enjoying a play at the theater.

The very rich — generally the big industrialists and developers — live in impressive mansions with swimming pools and gardens full of flowers and trees. They travel frequently, going abroad or to their vacation homes in the plush resorts of Acapulco or Cancún, Cuernavaca or Puerto Vallarta.

All the residents of Mexico City, rich and poor, share many of the problems and perils created by the city's size and continuing headlong growth. One of the worst is the chronic and horrendous air pollution. Mexico City's air is poisoned by 11,000 tons of solid-particle pollution every weekday. Of this, 70 percent comes from the exhausts of motorized vehicles. Another 15 percent is produced by 130,000 industrial enterprises large and small. The rest comes from so-called natural sources, including 750 tons per day of sun-dried human and animal waste, that mix with dust and blow in from the Neza area where filth collects in open sewers. And all this pollution often hangs in the air, immobile, because the mountains that surround the city cut off the breezes that might otherwise disperse some of the miasma.

During the May-to-September rainy season the frequent showers clear the air a little. Long holiday weekends that close the factories and reduce traffic also help. Then the citizens may glimpse the great volcanoes Popocatépetl and Iztaccíhuatl off to the southwest. These once constituted the city's chief scenic glory, something to which to lift the eyes, floating grandly above the urban turmoil like the Parthenon above Athens. Nowadays their sighting is a rare event, especially during the October-to-May dry season when the city is afflicted by winds strong enough to thicken the air with dust but too weak to blow away the smog. At the morning

2

Ready for work, young laborers lean
on a fence at a job mart near the
Zócalo, Mexico City's main square.
The signs advertise their skills in
electrical repairs, masonry and
painting, and their tool kits indicate
their willingness to work immediately.

rush hour, visibility may drop to less than three city blocks, and daytime instrument landings at the city's Benito Juárez airport are common.

This pollution is dangerous as well as annoying. Doctors say that 70,000 Mexico City residents a year die of pollution-related illnesses. Various pulmonary troubles kill many of them. Others succumb to parasitic diseases caused by airborne microorganisms that float in through kitchen windows or settle into less than hermetically sealed rooftop water tanks.

Government efforts to reduce industrial pollution have made little headway, in part because it remains cheaper and easier for factory owners to bribe inspectors than to install smoke scrubbers in their factory chimneys. Tax breaks for establishing factories elsewhere in Mexico have persuaded few entrepreneurs to move. Why build a

plant in Jalisco, they argue, only to ship most of its products back to Mexico City, which is by far the country's largest consumer market?

Efforts to lessen automotive pollution have so far been ineffective. There are simply too many vehicles in the city. By one recent count there were 200,000 buses, most of them rusty, clattering relics that spew clouds of black exhaust, plus 35,000 taxis, many equally ancient and inefficient. There were also more than 1.9 million private automobiles, almost all without emission-control equipment.

To make matters worse, Mexico City drivers are reckless consumers of fuel. Taking advantage of the fact that Mexican gasoline is cheap, they burn an average of 1,400 gallons per car each year, versus 578 gallons per car in the U.S. And Mexico City car engines burn all that fuel incompletely, in part be-

cause many automobiles are old, in part because the thin air at 7,350 feet requires a rich fuel mixture.

In consequence, the city's tail pipes pour out vast quantities of carbon monoxide, sulfur dioxide and lead, the last an insidious poison in which Pemex fuel is particularly high. Mexico City residents, says Javier Gutiérrez Baez, director of the Social Security Administration's occupational health laboratories, have four times as much lead in their systems as Mexicans elsewhere.

The flood of cars, taxis and buses also creates the city's world-famous traffic jams. Mexicans claim that during a visit to the capital, American astronaut Neil Armstrong remarked that it was easier to get to the moon and back than across Mexico City. The jams slow the average speed of downtown traffic to three miles an hour, not only increasing air pollution and raising the noise level to a deafening 90 decibels, but also creating delays that cost the economy 15 million work-hours a day.

The government has tried to ease the jams and the pollution by banning the manufacture by Mexico's auto industry of cars with eight-cylinder engines. There is little hope that this measure will help much. Large gas guzzlers can still be imported from the U.S., and Mexicans are endlessly ingenious at keeping old ones running.

Similarly, the government's efforts to ease the traffic problem by building freeways have not kept up with the city's proliferating vehicles. Built in the 1960s, a six-lane highway called the Periférico is so crowded at peak hours that traffic regularly slows to a crawl. To supplement and connect with it, the government in 1980 inaugurated a 75-mile system of high-speed avenues called *ejes viales,* or "axis roads," that now crisscross the capital city. These have reduced congestion in the residential areas somewhat, but they still funnel commuter traffic into the city's old, narrow downtown streets. To compound this downtown jam, the city is short an estimated 450,000 parking spaces, and double parking, although illegal, is endemic.

Even the swift and efficient metro system, which stretches octopus-like from the city center toward the teeming suburbs, has not solved many problems and has developed some of its own. At rush hour, baton-wielding police must be on hand to herd passengers through the subway stations and into the crammed cars like cattle, sometimes even separating the sexes "for reasons of modesty." "If we didn't," said one subway policeman, "you can't imagine the disorder that would take place."

The only bright spot in the traffic mess is that the jams do provide a market of sorts for a horde of unemployed men, women and children: These people circulate among the stalled cars wiping windshields, hawking newspapers and even staging fire-eating acts, with mouthfuls of kerosene spewed past lighted torches. So much a part of the everyday scene in Mexico City have these indefatigable street people become that a popular movie has been made about them.

Traffic as much as anything else has killed that treasured Mexican institution, the siesta. Too many people live too far from work to fight their way home and back during even a long lunch hour. Some have become exiled from sections of the city that they formerly enjoyed. "I haven't been downtown in three months," said architect José Ignacio Amor, whose offices are located in the south end of the city. An

Smartly uniformed traffic officers line up for inspection beside their vehicles. Women like these make up only a small part of the Mexican female work force, most of which is engaged in nonpaying jobs on family farms.

2

Enveloped in smog, the headquarters building of Petróleos Mexicanos (Pemex) rises above Mexico City. As air pollution has increased in the capital, daytime visibility has declined from an average of 10 miles in 1937 to seven and a half miles today.

Cars, buses and people jam a Mexico City intersection. To ease congestion, a subway system was opened in 1972; on 90 miles of track, it carries four million riders daily. But 200,000 buses and 35,000 taxis still bring the city to the verge of gridlock every rush hour.

urban researcher, María Eugenia Negrete, remarked, "I don't even have boyfriends in the northern part of the city. It's just not worth it to spend so much time on the Periférico."

As if pollution, noise and the frustration of the chronic transportation problems were not enough to vex its citizens, Mexico City's crime rate is rising with unemployment. According to newspaper reports, an armed robbery of some kind takes place every six minutes and there are on the average about 500 homicides a month, making Mexico City the world's most dangerous metropolis after New York.

Then there are long-standing problems of getting sufficient water into the city and getting its sewage out. The difficulty stems from the fact that the capital is on a semiarid plateau surrounded by rugged mountains. Some of the 55 tons of water that the city consumes every second must be pumped at great cost up over those mountains from springs and wells more than 100 miles away. The cost will continue to rise as more water must be brought in from still more distant sources.

A good portion of the sewage the city generates has to go out the same way the water comes in — over the mountains via a complex system of pumps, drainage canals and pipelines. "If our pumps ever fail," Raúl E. Ochoa, a director-general of the waterworks agency, has said, "we will all be swimming in sewage."

Similar pumps also go into action to remove excess water left by the cloudbursts that occasionally hit the city, not only flooding some of the more poorly drained suburbs, but also saturating the area's already spongy subsoil. This subsoil is mostly volcanic ash, unsuitable for bearing great weight under the best of conditions. The Aztecs had recognized long before the Spaniards came that their massive temples had a tendency to settle. The Spanish conquerors nevertheless built their own ponderous palaces and churches right on top of the rubble they had made of the Aztec city, which had been built in the middle of a lake that has for the most part disappeared.

This area remains the very center of the modern city, and the effects of the unstable ground beneath are not hard to find. Some of the older office buildings are badly out of plumb, and the great white-marble Palace of Fine Arts has slumped lopsidedly into the ground and will continue to do so as the soil beneath subsides eight inches a year. The fate of the city's modern high rises seems more assured, however, because of a technique pioneered by the American architect Frank Lloyd Wright. The 44-story Latin American Tower, for example, rests in part on 361 pilings that were driven 108 feet into the ground. The rest of the load is carried by a boxlike foundation 45 feet below the surface that floats on the muddy subsoil. The building has shown no signs of sinking, and it rode out the earthquakes of 1957 and 1985 without damage.

But architecture is the least of Mexico City's problems, and there is a growing suspicion that the entire city may eventually be doomed to founder in unimaginable chaos. Pessimists quote statistics to prove that should the number of automobiles in Mexico City continue to increase at the present rate, the entire road network would reach a saturation point well before the year 2000, making vehicular movement impossible. Others picture the city becoming literally uninhabitable, the water supplies fouled and the air unbreathable. A top government official has warned, "Catastrophe is not out of the range of possibility."

Javier Caraveo, Mexico City's first chief of urban planning and development, has readily agreed that the capital is desperately crowded. "All these people have no business being here," he once lamented. And he concedes that the growth of the metropolis cannot be halted but at best merely slowed

59

2

The country's most venerated shrine, the Basilica of the Virgin of Guadalupe in Mexico City, and its adjoining chapel are sinking into the spongy soil of what was once a lake bed. The old Basilica closed and a new one was consecrated across the way in 1976.

down. Nevertheless, he began in the early 1980s to implement some bold and ingenious remedies for the city's worst ills. Caraveo commenced by rerouting the buses, a measure that should sharply reduce pollution and also serve the people more efficiently. Until recently, privately owned bus companies were permitted to establish their own networks. The result was a spider web of 570 often redundant routes that overserved some areas and neglected others. Caraveo has put in effect a new system that will ultimately reduce the routes to 70, and these will cover the entire metropolitan area.

More ambitiously — and with the federal government's blessing — Caraveo has helped institute two forms of decentralization. One, it is hoped, will encourage urban growth in other, less densely populated parts of Mexico by making these new "poles of development" attractive enough to deflect citybound *campesinos* from moving to Mexico City. The federal government has made a start on this, decentralizing some of its bureaus. Mexico's various states, for example, will become responsible for their own educational systems, rather than having all authority — and a huge bureaucracy — reside in Mexico City.

The other decentralizing plan that Caraveo initiated in the early 1980s will divide Mexico City itself into nine new "urban centers" — self-contained cities within the city, each having its own business districts and housing areas, and each providing its own services and local mass transit. These urban centers will eventually be connected to one another by a larger and faster mass-transit network. "People will not have to travel as far or as often as they do now," Caraveo has said. "When they do need to

take a long trip, they will be able to do so quickly and relatively easily."

There are further plans to subdivide the urban centers into neighborhoods, where the residents will be involved in the decision-making process and thus in the future of their communities. These plans also call for parks and other green areas, to be carved out of the city's present chaos of new shantytowns and old decaying slums.

Such recipes for the future appear promising — if the needed funds are forthcoming from the Mexican government. The hope is that the government has finally been made sufficiently aware that inaction will almost surely bring disaster.

The citizens at any rate do seem to feel that their city's problems will somehow be solved. Bumper stickers on buses proclaim, "Mexico City, I believe in you," a statement that may be government propaganda but comes close to a consensus. "Mexico City," says lawyer Oscar Toledo gloomily, "is like a gigantic baby with an endless stomach demanding to be fed." But he adds in the next breath, "Mexico couldn't go on without Mexico City."

Anyone who is interested in sampling Mexico City enthusiasm should visit the Zócalo on the night of September 15, eve of Mexico's Independence Day. Crowded into this brightly floodlit 13 acres of pavement and into the nearby side streets are perhaps half a million people, standing shoulder to shoulder, waving Mexican flags, tooting incessantly on cardboard horns and tossing flour-filled eggshells and handful after handful of red, white and green confetti at one another.

Precisely at 11 p.m. the president of Mexico steps out onto a balcony of the long, three-story National Palace that

takes up the entire east side of the Zócalo. Tricolor sash gleaming across his white shirt front, he flourishes a Mexican flag just small enough for a man of normal strength to handle without difficulty. Above him hangs the great bell that Father Miguel Hidalgo y Costilla rang on September 16, 1810, to rouse a nation to throw off Spanish rule.

The bell begins to toll as the president cries out, in the words of that fiery priest, *"Viva México! Viva la independencia!"* Loudspeakers boom his words around the plaza, and the crowd roars them back at him. The same sound is also booming from every television set in Mexico City that happens to be operative and turned on; for this occasion they are joined in a single network. Now the president and the crowd sing the national anthem as he waves his banner back and forth and his fellow citizens in the square wave theirs.

The ceremony ends with fireworks, rockets arching high overhead while all around the square gigantic portraits of the heroes of independence blaze forth, etched in golden fire.

This boisterous celebration is a testament to the city's ability to survive its horrendous problems. It is a paradoxical place, growing and dying, sinking and rising at the same time, full of hope and despair in the middle of a country that is itself both rich and broke. Perhaps ultimately the city's survival will depend on the tough survivors that populate it, like 18-year-old Antonia Quiroz, who works as a chambermaid in a hotel from 5 a.m. to 9 p.m. six days a week and still finds time to study bookkeeping. "I live the best I can," she says simply. "We are in crisis, but I take it all with calm. The politicians work for their own interests, but we all hope for the future." □

Although it appears to have sunk into Mexico City's subsoil, this building, the gymnasium of a military academy, was actually built at an angle but has level floors inside. The architect's whimsy reflects the Mexicans' acceptance of the fact that many of the capital's buildings are listing.

A PLAZA'S VIBRANT LIFE

For all its size, Mexico City is a place of neighborhoods—each with its own character, its own civic administration, and more likely than not a central plaza that serves as a gathering spot for the inhabitants. Such is the case with Coyoacán, an ancient Indian city that has since become a residential district in the southwest part of town.

Coyoacán wears its local traditions with a rakish verve. During the Spanish conquest Hernán Cortés made his headquarters on the plaza; his palace still stands. In more recent times the area has taken on a mildly bohemian cast. The painter Diego Rivera lived there, as did the exiled Bolshevik Leon Trotsky, and today it is the favored quarter for writers, artists and entertainers. The plaza is at once park, marketplace, alfresco theater and outdoor living room. Residents stroll along its tree-shaded walks or gather at a nearby café. Vendors come to sell everything from tacos to live turkeys. And on weekends and fiesta days there are parades, dance performances and concerts sponsored by the local authorities. The result is a sense of community as strong and vibrant as in any country village in Mexico.

A panoply of flags for an Independence Day fiesta brightens Coyoacán's plaza, adorning the bandstand at left and the façade of Cortés' palace, which now houses local government offices.

Elaborately plumed Conchero dancers, who specialize in ancient Indian dance rites, perform for Coyoacán residents in front of the plaza's 16th-century San Juan Bautista church.

Two nuns sell religious articles in Coyoacán plaza to raise money for their order.

As families await a Sunday parade, a young pastry vendor prepares to set up his stand. Weekend entertainments sponsored by the authorities give the plaza a holiday air.

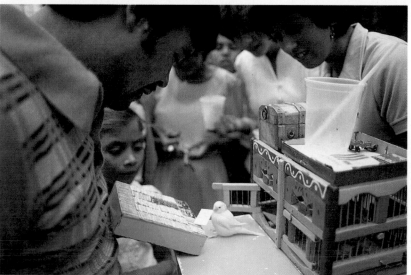

A fortunetelling canary plucks a message at random from a tray of inscribed cards — much to the delight of a youngster who has just handed over a few pesos to learn the future. Such avian oracles are standard features at street gatherings.

An open-front poultry shop just off
the square displays its wares and,
typically, a flower-bedecked altar
to the Virgin of Guadalupe, the
patroness of Mexico.

From a nearby market stall a visitor can quaff freshly blended fruit juice . . .

. . . order up a full repast of assorted seafood . . .

. . . or just snack on a taco stuffed with pork or beef.

Friday is market day in Coyoacán, and this Indian grandmother has come in from the country with her chickens and turkeys to set up shop on a side street near the plaza.

With long-practiced skill, a neighborhood folk artist stitches miniature dolls of her own design for sale at the Friday market. She has kept the same post, year in and year out, for as long as most residents can remember.

A matronly entrepreneur peddles brooms, dusters, dish towels, sponges and pot scrubbers on a sidewalk.

Tuning up for the evening show, a performer from a visiting pantomime troupe chats with a local shopkeeper about her company's scheduled run at one of Coyoacán's many theaters.

A municipal bandleader takes an audience request during a weekend fiesta in the plaza. The musicians are guest performers from another district, brought in to lend volume and variety to the festivities.

Several dozen life-size carved stone skulls stare out from a wall of the Great Temple, the major place of worship in the Aztec capital of Tenochtitlán, now Mexico City. Such macabre objects of veneration shocked the Spaniards when they first encountered the Aztec civilization in 1519.

THE GOLDEN INDIAN PAST

From the temple atop the pyramid of Tlatelolco on a sunny day in November 1519, Bernal Díaz del Castillo and a band of fellow Spaniards gazed in wonder upon an astonishing sight. Spread out before them, more or less on the site of present-day Mexico City, lay the Aztec capital, Tenochtitlán. Díaz was one of a company of a few hundred adventurers under the leadership of Hernán Cortés, a 34-year-old Spanish swashbuckler. Cortés and his men had landed on the Mexican coast eight months before; now a select few were at the temple at the northern end of the capital city and were being given a tour by the Aztec emperor Moctezuma II.

The city was like no other they had beheld. Built on marshland in the middle of a lake, it was bigger by far than their own capital of Seville. They could see below them a great arcaded market. To the south, in the heart of Tenochtitlán, soared the gleaming, lime-washed turrets of another temple complex. A section of royal palaces faced it, and beyond that spread 60,000 flat-topped adobe dwellings, neatly arranged along a network of well-kept streets and canals. Still farther away, three long causeways linked the city to the mountain valley. And on the horizon shimmered half a dozen other cities.

"We were amazed," recalled Díaz, who was the main chronicler among the Spaniards, "because of the lofty towers and buildings, all of masonry, rising from the water. Some of our soldiers even said that it must all be a dream."

Cortés and his expedition had set out from Cuba, where Spain had already established a colony, to explore the shores of the Gulf of Mexico. Initially Cortés had a written contract for the expedition, which he had negotiated with the Cuban governor, Diego Velázquez. But in the months that he spent making ready, Cortés managed to alienate a number of Cuban colonists, not least among them the governor himself. He strode about the Cuban capital, according to one Spanish account, "wearing a plume of feathers with a medallion and a chain of gold and a velvet cloak trimmed with gold," and attended by a large armed guard. He spent lavishly, recruiting men, purchasing supplies and assembling a fleet of about half a dozen ships.

Velázquez, who was jealous of his own authority, began to consider calling off the expedition. When Cortés got wind of the governor's second thoughts, he hurriedly ordered his men to embark, and they slipped out of the harbor on the morning of November 18, 1518. When Velázquez realized that his headstrong subordinate was gone, he issued orders for Cortés to be arrested, but it was too late.

Cortés made his way across the Gulf and touched ground on the Yucatán Peninsula in February or March of 1519. He and his men spent a few weeks sailing along the coast, doling out glass beads to the Indians and gather-

3

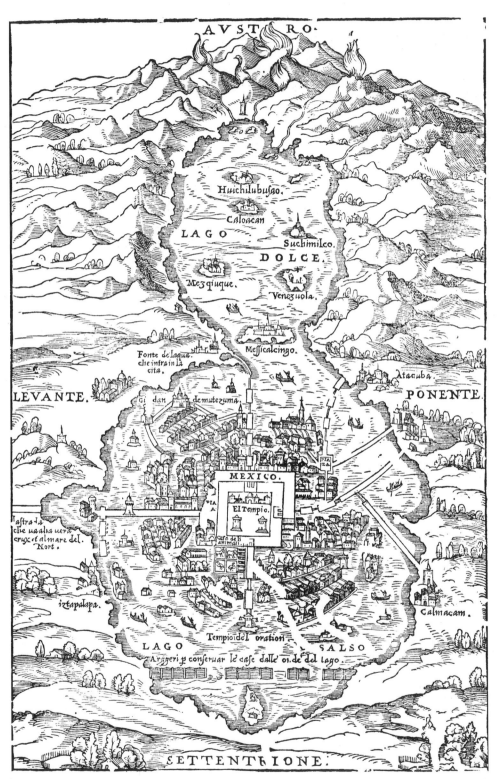

A 16th-century Italian map of the Aztec island city of Tenochtitlán shows the Great Temple that dominated the town center and the main causeways that led to the dry land of the valley around Lake Texcoco.

ing intelligence. Along the way, much to their amazement, they came upon a fellow Spaniard, Jerónimo de Aguilar, who had been shipwrecked off the coast of the Yucatán Peninsula eight years before and had since learned the Mayan language of the region. Aguilar joined Cortés and served as translator.

Cortés' good fortune was compounded when a Mayan chieftain welcomed him with gifts that included gold and 20 women, among whom was a princess who spoke Náhuatl, the language of the Aztecs in the interior. The Spaniards christened her Doña Marina, and her value to them would prove beyond reckoning. Doña Marina translated from Náhuatl to Maya, and Aguilar from Maya to Spanish. Eventually this remarkable woman would learn Spanish and be able to translate directly.

In April Cortés decided to head inland. But before doing so, he took it upon himself to found a colony. Planting a cross and a Spanish flag, he named the site Veracruz (True Cross) and ceremoniously claimed the land for Christianity and for Spain.

Moving cautiously into the interior, Cortés and his companions fought a few hostile tribes, but relied whenever possible on adroit diplomacy to win over the Indians. Many of the Indians gave the Spaniards a ready welcome; and wherever they went, they heard tales of the strength and splendor of the Aztec capital at Tenochtitlán.

Their arrival at the capital would bring a fateful confrontation between Europe and Indian America. It would lead in short order to the death of the emperor Moctezuma, the destruction of Tenochtitlán and the final collapse of the Aztec empire.

That empire — which stretched from the mountains in the north to the jun-

yliyocan.

gles of Tehuantepec in the south — was one of the world's most remarkable cultures. Its emperor received tribute from his scattered subjects, who paid him in gold and jewels, food and military services. Its cultural glories ranged from monumental architecture that could not have been built without the levying of thousands of workers, to the minutest calculations of movements of the heavenly bodies. It was a society that had been more than 2,000 years in the making and reflected a synthesis of the disparate achievements of other societies that had gone before it.

The Mexicans' earliest ancestors were nomadic hunter-gatherers who crossed the Bering Strait land bridge into North America about 30,000 years ago. From Alaska they filtered southward, and by 20,000 B.C. they had reached the area of modern-day Mexico City in the Central Valley. Archeologists have found traces of campfires, stone tools and the bones of the mammoths and mastodons they killed.

Sometime around 5000 B.C. these early Mexicans learned to farm. Their crops consisted of the same plants they had gathered as foragers — squash, chili peppers, beans and corn, which was protean in its uses. When dried, corn kept indefinitely, a matter of vital importance in a land where terrain and weather made agriculture uncertain. It could then be soaked in water and ground into meal, which could be further metamorphosed by being patted into a cake (the Spanish word "tortilla" means "little cake"). Once corn had been domesticated and crossbred to produce greater yields, it became the cornerstone of Mexican civilization.

Meanwhile, hunter-gatherers and farmers were spreading out over Mexico. Some went to the sweltering jungle marshlands of the Gulf Coast, an area that would hardly seem congenial to human habitation; and yet here it was that the Olmecs founded an urban culture of extraordinary complexity during the second millennium B.C.

The Olmecs arose on the Gulf shores of what are today the states of Veracruz and Tabasco. Of several dozen Olmec sites that have been found in Mexico, one ceremonial center at San Lorenzo in the state of Veracruz is among the oldest. Starting around 1200 B.C., the Olmecs buttressed the flanks of a broad clay plateau that rises 150 feet above the surrounding grasslands. Then, painstakingly hauling up basket after basket of soil onto the plateau, they raised mounds of earth, clustering them around rectangular courtyards that, for some unknown reason, they carefully aligned on a north-south axis.

Not the least impressive of San Lorenzo's features is a collection of seven gigantic stone heads (some of them nine feet tall) and 40-ton monolithic slabs adorned with fantastic animal and humanoid carvings. Having no stone in the area, the Olmecs had to quarry the rock in the Tuxtla Mountains, 50 miles away; and having neither the wheel nor draft animals, they had to wrestle it out of the quarry with nothing but ropes to aid human muscle. From the mountains they floated the stone by raft downriver to the Gulf of Mexico, then along the shore, and finally up another river to San Lorenzo, where it had to be hauled to the top of the plateau.

With variations, similar earthworks appeared in Olmec territory over the next 600 years. Some rose as high as 100 feet; many were elaborately paved with mosaics and adorned with altar blocks, stelae and colossal heads. They were often decorated with grotesque figures — human bodies with the faces of snarling jaguars. No one knows the significance of these figures. They may reflect a mythic descent from a jaguar god; one of the most remarkable shows a woman copulating with a jaguar-man. Whatever the symbolism, the jaguar appears repeatedly in Olmec statuary — and in the religious art made by other Indian societies throughout Mexico for hundreds of years after the Olmecs (for reasons also not known) had vanished from history.

No group of people embraced the Olmec legacy with such vigor or distinction as the Mayas, who flourished in southeastern Mexico and the area comprising today's Guatemala, Belize, Honduras and El Salvador. Their origins are obscure; but by 300 A.D. the Mayas deep in the rain forests of Guatemala had begun constructing elaborate

3

ceremonial centers reminiscent of those the Olmecs had built. The Mayas had one asset the Olmecs lacked — an abundance of limestone underlies the forest floor of the Petén region.

From there the Mayan civilization spread southeast into Honduras and northwest to the modern state of Chiapas in southern Mexico and later to the Yucatán Peninsula. Unlike the Olmecs, they left not only monuments, but also tantalizing clues as to how they lived. At Palenque in Chiapas, a lavishly carved stone crypt encloses the tomb of a king of the seventh century. His skeleton is ornamented from head to foot with jade necklaces, bracelets and rings. Such an elaborate burial suggests a ruling elite of great wealth and power.

The ceremonial nature of court life is evidenced at Bonampak, where the walls and ceilings of three rooms of a long stone building are adorned with brilliantly executed murals. One room shows nobles preparing for a sacred ritual; the second shows a war party making a raid on a neighboring tribe; and the third shows the execution and ritual sacrifice of the captives.

Despite the attention they paid to warfare, the Mayas also devoted energy to the arts and sciences. Mayan astronomers could calculate the phases of the moon, solar eclipses and the orbits of other heavenly bodies for centuries past and future. By Mayan reckoning, the present world began in the equivalent of 3114 B.C., and it replaced an earlier world. The calculations by which they figured back 3,000 years took account of leap years and depended on a solid grasp of mathematics.

The Mayan concern for recording time was matched by an urge to set down events. They carved hieroglyphs prolifically on their stone buildings and stelae, and inked them on paper made from pounded tree bark. From the few bark manuscripts that survive, linguists have discovered a pictorial writing system of at least 800 signs, used by the Mayas to mark names, birth dates, accessions to power, battles, deaths — an entire body of history. No other pre-Columbian culture had such command over abstract knowledge.

While the Mayas were living in the jungles of southeastern Mexico, a number of civilizations rose in the great Central Valley of Mexico, only to be supplanted periodically by nomads sweeping down from the arid highlands of the north. Among the last to arrive were the Aztecs, from a mysterious region they called Aztlán. They believed they were a chosen people whose tribal god, Huitzilopochtli, had promised to lead them to a site where they would find an eagle perched on a cactus, and there they should establish their homeland. "I shall make you lords and kings of whatever there is in the world, wherever it may be," he said.

The Aztecs arrived in the Central Valley around 1200. They drifted for a time among the established settlements, until they settled temporarily in an area of barren land infested with poisonous snakes. The Aztecs were a tough and determined lot; they ate the snakes and prospered.

They began to serve as vassals and mercenaries to the neighboring states, earning a reputation for valor and cruelty. On one occasion, they were hired by Coxcoxtli, chieftain of the city-state of Culhuacán, southeast of modern Mexico City, to help subdue a neighboring city-state. When they returned from battle, they had with them several thousand ears they had cut from the heads of slain enemies as trophies.

They also evidently outwitted Coxcoxtli, who was known for his craftiness. A legend tells how they persuaded him to give his favorite daughter in marriage to their chief, who promised to make her an Aztec queen. When the girl arrived in the Aztec camp, she was killed as an offering to Huitzilopochtli, in the expectation that as the god's bride she would become their goddess of war. Coxcoxtli, in a fury, summoned his warriors and drove the Aztecs from their settlements.

The Aztecs fled into the marshes of Lake Texcoco and hid among the reeds until Huitzilopochtli, so the story goes, came to their aid. He led them to a small island and there — just as he had promised — they found an eagle-like bird perching on a cactus. They built a temple and settled down for good. Thus, in the year 1345 the Aztecs founded Tenochtitlán, whose name in their tongue means "Place of the Cactus."

In many ways Tenochtitlán was an ideal spot for a settlement. The waters of the lake not only protected it from attack, but allowed for convenient transport of goods and provender. The lake also supplied fish, ducks and edible algae. The Aztecs ingeniously provided themselves with fertile farming land by scooping up the rich soil from the bottom of the lake and arranging plots among the shallows. There they planted corn, peppers, beans and squash in chinampas, or "floating gardens," so called because they seemed to be suspended in the lake.

Other Aztecs settled on the tiny adjacent isle of Tlatelolco and as the chinampas spread, the two islands became joined. By 1428 the Aztecs who lived on them had established themselves as the dominant power in the Central Valley.

Over the next 90 years the Aztecs embarked on a concerted policy of expansion. The most vigorous thrusts came during the reign of Moctezuma I, who ruled from 1440 to 1468 and carried the Aztecs to triumph on battlefields from Oaxaca to Veracruz.

As the Aztec empire gained in power and prestige, Tenochtitlán became the richest city in Mexico. Moctezuma I, who combined battlefield prowess with a talent for civic organization and artistic patronage, brought architects from Chalco, a city-state renowned for its buildings, to lay out the city's streets and canals and to beautify the city generally. For public buildings, adobe was replaced with stone. Gardens were planted. An aqueduct was built to pipe in fresh spring water.

Casting its shadow over life at Tenochtitlán and all the empire was the Great Temple pyramid of the god Huitzilopochtli, whose thirst for human blood was insatiable. Huitzilopochtli played a double role. Besides being the Aztecs' war-god, he was also the sun-god. By offering him a steady

The ruins of the Mayan city of Palenque glow against the foothills of the Sierra Madre de Chiapas. A terraced complex of stone temples surmounted by a four-story observation tower, Palenque was the Mayas' westernmost city — and was deemed sacred, as the place where the sun died.

RITUAL FIGURES FROM MAYAN GRAVES

Between 600 and 900 A.D., the island of Jaina, off the coast of Campeche, may have served the Mayans as a necropolis, a burial place for nobles and other dignitaries from the mainland. The island contains an immense graveyard, in which archeologists have found thousands of small clay figures like those shown here. Most of the statuettes — which represent gods and goddesses as well as men, women, children and animals — are whistles and rattles, and they may have been employed in ceremonies for the dead.

The inches-high figures — many of which bear traces of bright paint — suggest a deep love of ornamentation among the Mayan elite. They are adorned with jewelry, feathered capes, masks, elaborate headdresses and even tattoos.

An old sun-god embraces the moon-goddess. Mayas believed that the sun-god chased her daily across the sky.

A seated dignitary sports a mask and headdress that can be removed to reveal his face underneath.

The fickle moon-goddess takes a grinning rabbit for a consort. The Mayas saw a rabbit in the face of the moon, rather than a man.

Weaving cloth, a woman works at a loom that is attached to her waist and to a tree trunk. Such backstrap looms are still used by Mayan women.

Projecting power, a noble wears a necklace of jaguar teeth. Such teeth were believed to impart strength.

3

diet of human hearts, the Aztecs believed, they gave him souls to assist him in his daily passage across the heavens. The preferred victims were captives taken in battle.

The sheer number of these sacrifices is almost beyond imagination. When Moctezuma I's ambitious son Ahuítzotl came to the throne in 1468, he inaugurated his reign by ordering that the Great Temple of Huitzilopochtli in the center of the city be rebuilt on a massive scale and rededicated in an orgy of bloodletting. According to some accounts, 20,000 captives were marched up the temple steps to the stone altar, where priests cut into their rib cages and yanked out their still-beating hearts. The butchery lasted four days, from dawn to sundown.

Ahuítzotl subdued one Indian society after another, until the empire extended over more than 100,000 square miles — an area about the size of modern Italy. Within its bounds only a few ancient enemies, such as the Tlaxcalans, who dominated a valley about 60 miles to the east of Tenochtitlán, managed to cling to their independence.

In 1502, the throne passed to Mocte- zuma II — a nephew of Ahuítzotl and great-grandson of Moctezuma I — and he made it his first priority to collect tribute. He stationed imperial tax collectors throughout the empire to exact regular and prompt payments of cacao, cotton, feathers, precious stones, shells, jaguar skins, eagles, dyes, cloth, gold, silver, sandals and corn. The conscientiousness of these agents led to Moctezuma's own destruction, for his enemies would team up against him when Cortés arrived.

Moctezuma governed from atop a complex social structure. He was head

A MYSTERY RUIN IN THE VALLEY

Even for the Aztecs, Teotihuacán was a ghost city, a place that had come to such a sudden demise that they associated it with the end of one world and the beginning of another. Teotihuacán, which lies 35 miles northeast of Mexico City, covers nine square miles, and once was home to 200,000 people.

Not least among its imposing ruins are the 200-foot-high Pyramid of the Moon and the companion Pyramid of the Sun (right). Each was built with thousands of cubic yards of mud brick and faced with stone. For reasons unknown, Teotihuacán was destroyed by fire about 600 A.D.—probably by marauding nomads—and lost its preeminence as a trade center.

When the Spaniards arrived, in the 16th century, Teotihuacán had been deserted for nearly a millennium. The Aztecs—Moctezuma II included—held it in such awe that they made ritual pilgrimages there to worship among its ruins. Mystified by its origins, they ascribed its creation to the gods.

The eerie ruins of the Pyramid of the Sun—reflected here in the glass-smooth surface of rain water

priest, warlord and chief justice all in one. He held virtually absolute power, and was treated as a demigod. No subject was permitted to look him in the face, under pain of death.

Directly below him ranked the nobility, who enjoyed the privileges of commodious houses, servants, jewelry and income from war tribute and from farmland outside the city. In return they were expected to attend the emperor at court and to endure the occasional hardships of military campaigning. In theory, membership in the nobility was based on merit, particularly on valor in battle. But by the time of Moctezuma II, family status was beginning to count. The sons of noblemen attended elite schools designed to build character and to supply candidates for high positions in the priesthood, the government and the military — and the next generation of noblemen.

Special status was reserved for the priests, the earthly representatives of the gods. They were the custodians of writing, astronomy and astrology, medicine, and all Aztec lore. Priests ran the schools, where they taught their pupils law and government and drilled them in the spartan rigors of midnight hikes and ice-cold baths.

Next in rank came a small caste of traveling merchants, who grew rich on trading missions to outlying nations — often serving as imperial spies along the way. Below them were the ordinary citizens — artisans, shopkeepers, laborers and farmers — who lived in small adobe houses, could seldom afford to eat meat and might be called into battle at a moment's notice. They were forbidden to wear sandals or cotton garments. Cotton was an expensive import from what the Aztecs called the "hot-

lingering in the courtyard — give no hint of the thrumming activity that once marked this majestic city.

3

lands" — probably Guatemala — and so the poor had to content themselves with rude garments of agave fiber.

Lowest on the scale were the slaves, although slavery carried no irredeemable stigma. The mother of Itzcóatl, the emperor who had established the Aztecs' rule in the Central Valley, was a slave. Strange to say, most slaves were volunteers; a man might sell himself into bondage if his crops failed or if he had to pay off a debt, with the hope of buying his way out later on. Some slaves were prisoners captured in battle — but their slavery usually represented a temporary reprieve; most of them ended as human sacrifices at the temple.

The Aztecs demanded strict sobriety and obedience to law. Lying and theft were punishable by death, homosexuals were hanged, adulterers had their heads crushed between two stones, and slanderers had their lips cut off.

Moctezuma himself was a man of conflicting and enigmatic traits. He lived in a state of astonishing pomp and splendor. His household staff served him huge meals, which he ate alone behind a screen while being entertained by dancers, dwarfs and musicians. Yet Moctezuma had an ascetic streak, and on occasion he seemed more inclined to prayer and fasting than to pomp and luxury. Trained as a priest and steeped in astrological lore, he lived in a world full of portents — and allowed himself to be swayed by them.

In the first two decades of the 16th century, a series of startling events gave him reason to worry. One night a gigantic comet lit the sky. And then, on a windless day, an enormous wave rose out of Lake Texcoco and caused destruction all along the shore. Another time, a small temple burned mysteriously to the ground. To Moctezuma's

superstitious mind, all these events combined to portend that some great upheaval was at hand.

Indeed it was. Early in 1519 a messenger arrived breathless from the Gulf region with news that tall ships had been sighted off the coast. The ships belonged to the expedition led by Cortés, and reports of its progress poured in to Moctezuma's court. As the ships sailed up the coast from the Yucatán Peninsula to the area of Veracruz, Indian scouts tracked them every bit of the way. Now and then the creatures that lived aboard came ashore, and they were stranger even than the ships. White-skinned, bearded, clad in suits of shining metal that seemed impervious to Indian arrows, the beings carried sharp-edged weapons that gleamed like silver in the sunshine; other weapons spouted fire and smoke, and the most terrible of these could shatter a tree into splinters.

Then there were the animals: huge dogs with burning yellow eyes and jaws dripping saliva, and — most fearsome of all — a monstrous beast that seemed to be half man and half deer, tall as a house, and that shook the ground when it ran, "as if stones were raining on the earth," said an Indian chronicler. Such was the Aztecs' first impression of a horse and rider.

To Moctezuma and some of his countrymen, these creatures seemed to be not men, but deities. Perhaps, reasoned Moctezuma optimistically, they were emissaries preparing the way for Quetzalcóatl, god of the morning star, who in ancient times had been forced by a rival god to flee to the East but had promised to return.

As the Spaniards under Cortés marched inland over the mountains, the news reaching Moctezuma gave less and less reason for optimism. At Tlaxcala, city of the Aztecs' most formidable foe, the warriors came out to do battle and were quickly routed. Cortés entered the city, made peace with its ruler and continued on — reinforced by several thousand Tlaxcalan fighting men.

At Moctezuma's court, this turn of

Aztec priests sacrifice two captives to the god Huitzilopochtli. To be sacrificed was an honor, and prisoners accepted such a fate stoically, referring to their captors as "fathers." After the heart was cut out, the body was often beheaded and the skin removed, to be worn by a priest for 20 days.

events plunged the empire into crisis. What should Moctezuma do? If the newcomers were gods, he must propitiate them; if they were men bent on conquest, he must stop them. But how? The Spaniards' weapons carried a death-dealing magic beyond any in Moctezuma's experience, and the ease with which they gathered allies from among Aztec enemies was worse yet. Moctezuma, hearing of the visitors' lust for gold, sent relays of messengers with sacks full of it — little realizing that, far from buying the Spaniards off, the gold only lured them onward.

All Moctezuma's courage seemed to drain from him. "What will become of us?" he is recorded as saying. "Once I was happy, but now I have death in my heart." He arranged an ambush at Cholula, a city in the present-day state of Puebla. The Spaniards were to be greeted amicably, bedded down and then murdered in their sleep. Doña Marina got wind of the plot, through a friendly Indian woman, and duly alerted her Spanish benefactor. Cortés promptly massacred the Cholulans.

The Spaniards continued on their way, an Aztec chronicler noted, marching "in battle array, as conquerers, and the dust rose in whirlwinds on the roads. Their spears glinted in the sun, and their pennants fluttered like bats." And so, on November 8 of 1519, the fearsome host arrived at the threshold of Tenochtitlán.

The Aztec court was now in a turmoil of quarrelsome indecision. Some of Moctezuma's advisers, most notably a brother named Cuitláhuac, urged him to call out his warriors and put up a stiff resistance. But the emperor — either having concluded that resistance was useless, or perhaps still uncertain about the nature and the intentions of the ar-

rivals — decided to give them a welcome fit for gods.

At his behest, a delegation of 4,000 Aztec nobles met the Spaniards on a causeway to the city and offered garlands of flowers. Then came the emperor himself, shaded by a canopy of shimmering green feathers, pearls and silver threads. As he walked, his retainers carpeted the road with their mantles so that the gem-encrusted gold sandals of the imperial feet would not have to touch the earth.

Moctezuma offered Cortés a pair of necklaces, each hung with eight enormous gold pendants fashioned to look like shrimp. He had the Spaniards escorted to quarters in the palatial residence that had belonged to his father and inundated his guests with gifts. That first afternoon he delivered 5,000 embroidered cotton tunics, along with baskets full of elaborate featherwork, and gold and silver jewelry. "In all the land that lies in my domain you may command as you will," he said through the interpreters Doña Marina and Aguilar, "and all that we own is for you to dispose of as you choose."

Historians ever since have speculated as to why Moctezuma, who ruled his own people so sternly and arrogantly, should have been so ready to relinquish his realm to the Spaniards. One theory is that the Spaniards, with their strange appearance, their fearsome weapons and their evident invincibility, still seemed to be gods. Another is that Moctezuma, as a practical man and an experienced warrior, saw surrender as the better part of valor. Yet a third is that he may have thought he would stand a chance of outwitting them if he appeared to make them welcome within his own precincts.

Whatever the explanation, the Span-

iards made themselves quite at home, and each new sight brought a deeper sense of wonder. Exploring the palace gardens, they marveled at the profusion of rare flowers and herbs. Near the gardens were the royal aviaries — thousands of birds of all species, with artificial ponds for the ducks and herons, and a force of 300 keepers to attend them. There was also a royal zoo for carnivores and reptiles that included rattlesnakes, which "carry on their tails things that sound like bells," the chronicler Díaz wrote. When the "jackals and foxes howled and the serpents hissed," he went on, "it seemed like a hell."

Quite apart from such exotica, the sheer physical grandeur of the city was astonishing to the Spaniards. Its streets were kept spotless by an army of sweepers, its handsome houses were bedecked with rooftop flower gardens, and dominating all was the vast pyramid of the Great Temple, which was of a "size and magnificence no human tongue could describe," Cortés wrote to the Spanish king.

A few days after the Spaniards' arrival, Moctezuma led a party to the pyramid of Tlatelolco at the northern edge of the city to view the panorama that would so enthrall Díaz. Along the way they paused in the Tlatelolco marketplace, which was a marvel of organization. Each commodity was assigned its own sector. There was an area for jade, another for lumber, others for limestone and for salt. One street was reserved for herbalists, another for barbershops, another for dealers in wild ducks, turtledoves, parrots, eagles, owls and sparrow hawks. There was a butchers' quarter that offered hare, venison and, reported Díaz, "small gelded dogs that they breed for eating." Some traders dealt only in cacao beans, which

83

3

were so highly prized that they were commonly used as money; only the nobility could afford to drink chocolate.

Díaz showed particular interest in the gold exchange. The grains of gold were placed in goose quills "so that the gold can be seen through, and according to the length and thickness of the quills they arrange their accounts," he wrote. If a dispute developed as to quality or amount, the customer could seek a decision from a board of judges seated nearby in a pavilion. Other officials patrolled the marketplace to make sure that no one cheated.

At the far end of the marketplace rose the pyramid with its temple. Díaz

Standing atop his palace in this 16th-century painting, Moctezuma II spots a comet, which he took for an omen. The artist was an Indian employed by Spanish missionary Father Diego Durán to record Aztec life.

Tall-hatted Spanish soldiers crowd the decks of a ship as one of their companions fishes near the shore. From a perch in a treetop, an Aztec sentry observes the Spaniards' arrival.

Five Aztec warriors carrying javelins and shields besiege armor-clad Spaniards inside the palace where Moctezuma quartered the visitors.

counted 114 steps as the men climbed to the top. There, the emperor pointed out the sights of the city. Then he led the Spaniards into the temple.

Suddenly their fascination turned to horror. A pair of enormous idols loomed in the murk of the interior. One was Huitzilopochtli; the other was Tezcatlipoca, god of darkness.

The idol that most caught their eye was the one representing Huitzilopochtli. "It had a very broad face and

monstrous, terrible eyes," Díaz wrote, "and the body was girdled by great snakes made of gold and precious stones." But the idol itself was the least of the horror. Beneath it, Díaz went on, "were some braziers with incense that they call copal, and in them were burning the hearts of three Indians whom they had sacrificed that day. All the walls of the oratory were so splashed and encrusted with blood that they were black . . . and the soil so bathed with it that in the slaughterhouses of Spain there is not such another stench."

Cortés, incredible as it may seem, chose to deliver a brief lecture on the merits of Christianity. "Señor Moctezuma," he began, according to the Díaz chronicle, "surely a great and wise prince like yourself must understand that these idols of yours are not gods, but devils. . . . Let me place a cross here at the top of this tower, and set up an image of Our Lady, and you will see by the fear in which these idols hold it that they have been deceiving you."

The emperor listened to the Spaniard in diplomatic silence, but his eyes hardened. "I should never have shown you my gods," he declared. "They give us health and rains and good seed times and seasons and as many victories as we desire. I pray you not to say another word to their dishonor."

Such a statement conveyed nuances that reinforced an uneasiness the Spaniards felt despite the lavish treatment they had been receiving at the hands of the Aztecs. "We walked," Díaz recorded, with "our beards always over our shoulders." The Aztecs' veiled unfriendliness was doubly worrisome because Tenochtitlán was potentially a military trap. The wooden bridges leading to the city could be severed to keep people on the island or off it, as

THE MAGNIFICENT STONE OF THE SUN

Of the thousands of artifacts that reflect the complex thinking and creative vigor of the Aztecs, few are more imposing than the sculptured basalt disk that is sometimes known as the Stone of the Sun (*above*). A monumental 12 feet in diameter and 26 tons in weight, it once adorned the Great Temple of Huitzilopochtli in the central square of Tenochtitlán. It depicts in intricately carved relief the Aztecs' cosmos — their gods, their cultural rites and the dates by which they reckoned time.

Scholars have yet to decipher all its mysteries. But most agree that the glowering face in the central medallion represents the sun-god. The two ear-shaped cartouches on either side of it show claws clutching hearts, reminiscent of the Aztecs' grisly rite of human sacrifice. The four rectangular cartouches surrounding the sun-god portray gods representing (*counterclockwise from upper right*) the elements of earth, wind, fire and water — which, the Aztecs believed, had each in turn destroyed four previous "worlds" or epochs in history antedating their own.

In concentric bands around those figures are hieroglyphic representations of months and years extending back to the beginning of the present world — given as 1011 A.D. Girdling the whole are two snakes, their heads confronting each other at the base and their tails meeting at the top.

The Spaniards, in a frenzy of Christian piety, cast the disk into the rubble of the magnificent city they destroyed. It remained in limbo until 1790, when treasure hunters inspired by lingering tales of Aztec wealth found it while digging in the Zócalo. Today Mexicans, increasingly proud of their Indian heritage, have it prominently displayed at the National Museum of Anthropology in the capital's Chapultepec Park.

3

the case demanded. Should trouble flare with the emperor's warriors, the Spaniards could be held there.

When word came that six Spaniards on the coast had been killed by subjects of Moctezuma, Cortés had a golden opportunity to change the status quo in Tenochtitlán. With a bodyguard of 30 Spaniards, he betook himself to Moctezuma. "I do not wish to begin a war on this account, nor to destroy this city," Díaz says he told the emperor. "I am willing to forgive it all if silently, and without raising any disturbance, you will come with us to our quarters, where you will be well served and attended. But if you cry out or make any disturbance you will immediately be killed by these, my captains, whom I brought solely for this purpose." Moctezuma meekly went along — and found himself under house arrest in the quarters he had given the Spaniards.

Cortés had no sooner achieved that coup than he had another problem to contend with. Word came that a large force of Spanish soldiers had landed at Veracruz with orders from the Cuban governor to apprehend him; and they were now tracing his footsteps inland. Moctezuma was delighted, for it seemed that he himself would be miraculously delivered of his captor. He did not reckon, however, on the resolve and daring of the Spanish captain. Cortés appointed a lieutenant, Pedro de Alvarado, to keep an eye on Moctezuma with some of the Spanish troops. Cortés gathered the rest of the men and sped toward the coast, picking up volunteers from among the Indians he had earlier befriended.

He found his adversary at Cempoala, about 70 miles inland from Veracruz. He arrived under cover of darkness and surprised the Spanish commander,

who quickly surrendered with all of his troops. Cortés then marched back to Tenochtitlán — the hundreds upon hundreds of soldiers who had come to capture him eagerly joining his force in the expectation of booty.

What he found at the capital filled him with dismay. Some Aztec nobles had held a religious celebration in the temple courtyard and Alvarado, fearing an attack on himself, had turned on the celebrants and slaughtered them. In outrage, the inhabitants of Tenochtitlán rose up against the Spaniards and besieged them in the palace. Only the presence of Moctezuma, whom Alvarado still held under house arrest, prevented their capture.

The city was ominously quiet when Cortés arrived. He now made a grievous mistake. He led his troops unopposed through the streets and into the palace — only to find himself and his

men encircled by a horde of Aztec warriors. Each attempt to break out was met by a savage barrage of flint-tipped arrows and stone missiles. Cortés dragged Moctezuma onto the palace roof and ordered him to quiet his people. It was no use. A stone hurled from below struck the Aztec ruler in the head, and three days later he died.

The siege went on, and Cortés grew desperate. With food and powder running short, and his men badly mauled by continued enemy assaults on the palace gates, he had to escape somehow. The Aztecs had removed the bridges that spanned the canals, so Cortés had his soldiers construct a portable bridge to carry with them. In the small hours of July 1, 1520, with the city shrouded in fog, and with their horses' hoofs wrapped in cloth to muffle the sound, the Spaniards crept out of the palace and made for the edge of the city.

They reached the first canal undetected, set up the bridge and crossed onto a causeway. But an old woman was drawing water from the canal and, looking up, she saw the moving troops. She let out a cry, and the Aztec sentries took up the alarm, trumpeting on conch shells. Thousands of warriors materialized in minutes. Some attacked from canoes in the canal; others swarmed onto the causeway and mercilessly knifed the fleeing Spaniards.

A handful of Spaniards still managed to make their way to the second canal, but their portable bridge collapsed under the weight of the men and horses. Now they jumped into the water and tried to wade. Since many of them on leaving the palace had loaded themselves down with Aztec gold, they stumbled in the water. Soon the canal was a thrashing tangle of wounded and drowning men and horses.

Eventually Cortés and his sadly diminished forces gained solid ground and regrouped at the foot of a giant tree. More than 1,000 Spaniards had set out from the palace, and at least 450 of them were now dead, along with 4,000 of Cortés' Indian allies. The debacle would go down in Spanish history as *La Noche Triste* — the Night of Sorrows. The generally emotionless Cortés, so tradition goes, sat under the tree and wept.

In the Aztec capital, the victory was celebrated by the installation of a new emperor, Moctezuma's brother Cuitláhuac, the one who from the first had urged the Spaniards' expulsion. Cuitláhuac assessed his forces and deemed them strong enough to meet any assault. But he did not take into account a silent scourge that the Spaniards had brought with them to the Central Valley — smallpox. Aztecs died from the disease by the tens of thousands. Cuitláhuac was among the dead, and he was succeeded by Moctezuma's 18-year-old cousin Cuauhtémoc, whose name means "Falling Eagle." Brave and determined, the new emperor prepared to meet the anticipated Spanish onslaught by gathering conscripts and volunteers from allies far and wide, and training them relentlessly.

Cortés, however, had led his remaining men to Tlaxcala, where he gathered a fresh army of Indian troops. Ten months later he marched back to the edge of the city at the head of a large force. It included 500 troops, together with their arms, horses and 18 cannon of bronze and cast iron, sent by the governor of Cuba in a further attempt to stop Cortés; once again the irrepressible commander had won his would-be captors over to his side. Nearly 100,000 Indian foot soldiers from Tlaxcala and Texcoco swelled the ranks Cortés commanded. Remembering the painful lesson of the causeways, he had built a number of sailing craft, which were hauled in sections over the mountains; he would control the lake, and with it access to Tenochtitlán.

The collapse of the city now seemed inevitable. Cortés cut the aqueducts that brought in drinking water, and with his boats he set up a blockade to halt the food supply. Soon the citizens were reduced to eating lizards and tanned hides. Still, they put up a fierce resistance. They stationed themselves on the rooftops, and every time the Spaniards and their allies tried to enter the city they were turned back by a fusillade of projectiles from above.

Cortés was nothing if not resourceful, and he found a wicked way to defeat the Indians' defense. Hauling his cannon onto the causeways, he proceeded to blast the Aztecs' buildings into rubble. Detachments of men then moved into the streets and systematically leveled the buildings one by one, giving the Spaniards room to maneuver. The palaces were brought down; so were the gardens and the zoo, and the soaring architecture in the Great Temple square. The invaders pushed steadily onward, forcing the Aztecs back into Tlatelolco — site of the pyramid from which they had beheld the panorama of the capital city. Soon that too was overrun, and the temple was burned.

Our cries of grief rise up
and our tears rain down,
for Tlatelolco is lost.
The Aztecs are fleeing across the
lake;
they are running away like women.

Thus wrote an Aztec poet after the event, and another poet plaintively asked the god Tezcatlipoca:

Have you grown weary of your
servants?
Are you angry with your servants,
O Giver of Life?

Even the brave young emperor Cuauhtémoc took flight; he was captured while fleeing in a canoe on the afternoon of August 13.

When taken to Cortés to surrender, he touched the dagger in the Spaniard's belt. "I have done everything in my power to defend myself and my people, and everything that it was my duty to do," he said. "Kill me, for that will be best." Instead Cortés kept him prisoner. But two years later, on hearing a rumor that the erstwhile emperor was plotting an uprising, he had Cuauhtémoc hanged.

So fell the last of the Aztec emperors, and the venerable Aztec civilization. Mexico now entered a phase of vassalage to Spain, half a world away. □

This 14th-century statue — in its original colors — was uncovered at an entrance to the Great Temple in Mexico City after serious excavation began in 1978. Such reclining figures are believed to represent messengers between the priests and the gods.

Paper figures depict the birth of Christ in a hand-lettered book on Otomí religious practices that mingles Christian and pagan elements.

VILLAGE WITH A LIVING PAST

In a misty valley 120 miles northeast of Mexico City—a refuge so secluded that until the 1970s it was accessible only by foot or on horseback—is an Indian village where ancient ways not only survive but prosper. This is San Pablito, home to about 2,500 Otomí, who continue to speak their own language among themselves. The villagers are pious Catholics, but they also support several shamans, through whom they pay homage to a pantheon of more than a dozen major spirits and innumerable minor ones.

The foundation of San Pablito's prosperity is a special paper, handmade of rock-pounded bark. It is used by the inhabitants in their rites, and one shaman makes religious books from it, illustrating them with cutouts *(left)*. But most of the paper is shipped from the town and sold for artistic purposes. Because of the demand for it, virtually every inhabitant practices the 2,000-year-old craft of making paper. Indeed, the sound of the papermakers at work reveals the presence of the village to an approaching visitor, for the pounding of rocks on bark echoes throughout the valley.

Three men of San Pablito walk past an *oratorio,* **or shrine, still used in rites of the ancient Otomí religion. The villagers, while clinging to old ways, nevertheless welcomed electricity and the outdoor plumbing that brought them running water.**

After mass, a visiting priest will bless water in the vessels before the altar so that parishioners can carry it to their homes for religious use.

A volunteer, one of many who
maintain the church, scrubs the floor.
Although it is visited by a priest
only sporadically, the church is
carefully kept up and is provided
with fresh flowers as well as garlands
of cutout paper flowers.

A volunteer, one of many who
maintain the church, scrubs the floor.
Although it is visited by a priest
only sporadically, the church is
carefully kept up and is provided
with fresh flowers as well as garlands
of cutout paper flowers.

Wearing the red-sashed cotton skirt
and embroidered blouse that make
up the traditional costume of Otomí
women, a worshipper genuflects
before a statue of the Virgin Mary
clothed in Indian garb.

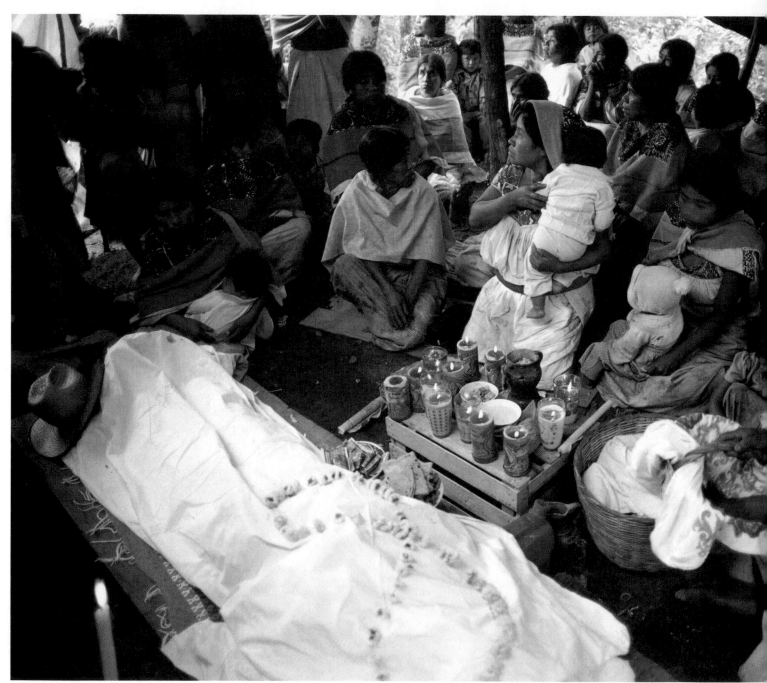

Mourners gather at a bier on which, in the ancient way, marigolds, food, money and a hat have been arrayed. These are intended for use in the hereafter

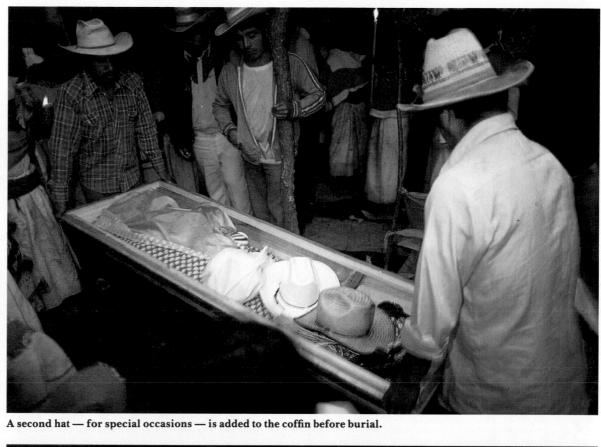

A second hat — for special occasions — is added to the coffin before burial.

In evening darkness, the ornate coffin, brought from a city an hour's travel away, is lowered into the grave.

A woman arranges the grid of fig-bark fibers that she will pound with a hand-size rock to make paper. The boy is smoothing a pounded sheet.

THE SACRED PAPER OF SAN PABLITO

Historically, Mexican Indians have endowed paper with religious significance, using it for sacred books, ceremonial dress, altar decorations, temple banners and in sacrifices. Today it still has spiritual meaning to the Indians of San Pablito.

The raw material for the villagers' paper is the inner bark of fig trees. After being dried, the bark is cut into strips several feet long, soaked, then boiled in caustic limewater (the solution used for processing corn for tortillas) to separate it into fibers. The fibers are laid out on a smooth board in a grid (left) and beaten with flat lava rocks until the grid spreads into a sheet, which is finally dried in the sun.

Much of the paper goes to the tourist trade. A few of the inhabitants paint pictures on it to sell, and the dazzling paintings of the Guerrero Indians are also made on it. But some is always held back for the shamans to employ in their ancient religious rites (overleaf), where more colorful machine-made tissue paper is also used.

A shaman cuts spirit figures from folded paper to use in the production of holy books.

Figures are pasted under religious text, carefully written by hand.

A shaman sprinkles the blood of a
sacrificial chicken onto paper figures
representing evil spirits to be
exorcised from a visitor. By using such
offerings as liquor and cigarettes, the
shaman hopes to lure the spirits to
their own images and thus trap them.

Gathered in remembrance, Mexicans wait for the annual celebration of the 1910 revolution to begin. Above the crowd are portraits of revolutionary heroes: from left to right, Aquiles Serdán, Francisco Madero, Pancho Villa and Emiliano Zapata.

THE STRUGGLE FOR LAND AND LIBERTY

"Formerly we were at the end of the world, and now we are in the middle of it, with an unprecedented change in our fortunes." So wrote the Spanish humanist Hernán Pérez de Oliva, as word of the great events in the New World spread through Spain in the early 1520s. "Well then, gentlemen, take advantage of the great fortune that is now coming to Spain," Pérez went on, "and you will have opened for yourselves a road by which you can participate in this fortune, and bring to your families great prosperity."

Pérez de Oliva's attitude reflected the general sense of jubilation, pride and hope for the future felt throughout Spain. King Charles V quickly forgave Hernán Cortés for his insubordination and named him governor and captain general of the new colony. In the next several years Spaniards by the shipload sailed for New Spain, as the colony was called; they were eager to exploit the newfound wealth that was evidenced by Moctezuma's elaborate city.

They did not confine themselves to Tenochtitlán. Within two or three decades Spaniards had explored more than a million square miles of territory that reached across Mexico from the Gulf to the Pacific, south to the Yucatán Peninsula and north into present-day Texas, Arizona, New Mexico and California. And in the process they claimed suzerainty over the estimated 25 million Indians who lived there.

Out of the fierce clash of Spanish and Indian cultures was to come a new amalgam, the nation of Mexico. But that nation would be four long centuries in the making and would emerge from a crucible of bloodshed and misery. In its first three centuries, the colony existed at the pleasure of the Spanish Crown. The fourth century was beset by continual wars; the Mexicans fought for liberation from Spain, then for freedom from foreign meddling; finally they struggled among themselves in a decade-long revolution to resolve the inequities and hatreds that were the legacy of colonial rule.

The seeds of trouble were sown at the very start. Cortés and his fellow conquistadors lost no time in stamping out the remains of the Indian heritage; within six months of their conquest, Mexico City began taking shape on the ruins of Tenochtitlán, to become the capital of New Spain. A cathedral rose near the site of the old temple of Huitzilopochtli. Nearby was erected a palace where Cortés, and after him a long line of Spanish viceroys, would reside in feudal splendor.

The transplanted Spaniards received no pay from the Crown for their work; they were expected to share the booty that was left after the greater part of the Aztec treasure had been set aside for the king. When the gold and jewels from Moctezuma's palace had been divided, Cortés — with the somewhat reluctant approval of the authorities in Spain — distributed among his men

Nahua

Maya

Tarahumara

some of the 370 towns that had paid tribute to the Aztec emperor. The bequests were known as *encomiendas* — entrustments. The Indians who lived in them were required to pay annual tribute of food and goods to their new Spanish overlords — and, in addition, to furnish free labor. Through such grants Cortés (who took 22 *encomiendas* along with 23,000 Indian vassals for himself) and other early settlers became the richest men in the entire Spanish empire. They looked forward to a long and relatively independent rule over their fiefdoms.

Within a few years, however, the conquistadors faced unwelcome rivals in the continuing quest for wealth and prestige. Cortés himself fell out of favor with Charles V, who wanted no challenge to his authority in the New World. In 1535 the king sent a royal kinsman, Don Antonio de Mendoza, to supplant Cortés as governor. Cortés returned to Spain, hoping to reclaim his title and his standing; the effort failed, and he died there in 1547, fabulously

rich but frustrated and embittered.

Over the next 250 years, more than 300,000 Spaniards crossed the ocean to New Spain. Foremost among them were those who came as ranking appointees of the Crown — viceroys, judges, high army officers — or to serve the church as bishops. Although they might spend the better part of a lifetime in New Spain, they continued to look upon themselves as Spaniards — or *peninsulares*, a reference to the Iberian Peninsula. Yet, in spite of their disinclination to put down roots, they formed the ruling class — and a wealthy one. Together with their offices they frequently received grants of land that included the Indians who resided on it. They could add to their holdings by buying land at low prices from the

Crown. One Spanish *marqués* acquired 222,000 acres for a mere 250 pesos — half the price of a horse.

Other Spaniards came hoping that in the New World they would find the material wealth and the rank that Spanish society denied them. These men, too, could buy land cheaply, and some of them bought enough of it to establish haciendas — plantations of cotton, corn, sugar, wheat and sisal; others undertook to mine silver from rich lodes in the northern highlands. In staying permanently, such entrepreneurs gave rise to two other classes. The progeny of those who brought wives from Spain were known as *criollos*. To the extent that they were of pure Spanish descent, the *criollos* identified themselves with the *peninsulares*. Some became mer-

Mexico is a land of rich ethnic diversity. These Indians represent the dozens of subcultures that survive there today, each having its own language.

chants and lesser civil servants; a great many joined the clergy and as parish priests, monks and teaching brothers enjoyed the bonanza of exemption from state taxation and civil trial. But neither the church nor the state gave the *criollos* any real power, and the highest appointments were generally made from abroad.

The offspring of Spaniards who mated with Indians were *mestizos* (of mixed blood), as were the offspring of those who mated with the 150,000 Africans who for a brief spell in the early

Huave

1600s were imported to work as slaves in the cotton fields. *Mestizos* might aspire to wealth, but they seldom held political office.

Below the *mestizos* there were the Indians, whom the Spaniards looked upon as wards of the church and the state. Some of them learned to speak Spanish, and most took to worshipping in the Spaniards' churches. But they provided what amounted to slave labor on the haciendas, in the mines and in the textile factories. Those who worked the fields toiled from sunup to sundown in debilitating heat. The miners often had to make two-week journeys on foot to get to the sites and then had to find their own food and shelter when they arrived. And the textile workers were sometimes locked in at their looms for 24 hours at a stretch.

Thus, from as early as the second generation after the conquest, Mexico had within its borders four classes with separate identities — whose irreconcilable interests inevitably led to festering grievances. The *peninsulares* looked

Zapotec

down on the *criollos* for having been born in the New World. The *criollos* resented the *peninsulares* for their superior airs and came to call them *gachupines* — wearers of spurs. (Spurs, a costly affectation of Spanish gentlemen, were conspicuous in a land where the local population generally adopted the Indian practice of riding bareback.) The *mestizos,* as the products of two cultures, belonged to neither. The pure-blooded Indians stood hopelessly at the bottom of the social structure and felt that those above them had robbed them of their land and their traditions.

Despite the sharply drawn lines, all four classes lived together more or less in peace, and the colony prospered. By the end of the 18th century it was producing half of the world's silver and providing two thirds of Spain's revenues. The total number of residents in New Spain was approaching six million. About 58 percent were Indians, 25 percent *mestizos,* 17 percent *criollos* and less than one quarter of 1 percent *peninsulares.* Practically all land and wealth were held by the white upper

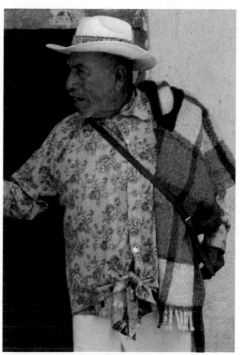

Otomí

101

4

class — the 15,000 *peninsulares* and the *criollos*. It seemed to a contemporary bishop that there were in reality only two groups: "those who have nothing and those who have everything." And to Friedrich Heinrich Alexander Baron von Humboldt, a German naturalist who passed through Mexico on a five-year tour of the New World, the distinction appeared to be one purely of color. "A white, even if he rides barefoot on horseback, considers himself a member of the nobility of the country," von Humboldt wrote.

Nevertheless, increasing numbers of *criollos* were becoming estranged from the mother country. Besides resenting the superior airs of the *gachupines,* they resented taxes levied on their properties and they longed for a voice in governing their own affairs. And so the first cracks in this rigid economic and social order appeared not among the teeming masses who were exploited, but among discontented *criollos* — priests, teachers and a few military officers who were generally well-to-do and literate but politically powerless. They were inspired by the successful revolutions in France and in Britain's North American colonies and encouraged by the fact that the mother country was in desperate straits. In 1808, Napoleon Bonaparte invaded Spain and took the king prisoner. With the interruption of direction from the Spanish Crown, the *criollos* began hatching plots to overthrow Spanish rule.

Altogether, more than 100 conspiracies and rebellions occurred during the colonial period, but they all lacked leadership and quickly fizzled out. No real independence movement got under way until the rise of Miguel Hidalgo y Costilla, a middle-aged priest in the parish of Dolores in the west-central part of the colony. Hidalgo, who was a *criollo* by birth and pro-Indian by sentiment, was as concerned with teaching his Indian flocks how to plant vineyards, grow silk and tan hides as he was with teaching the catechism. When not thus engaged with his Indian parishioners he took part in a so-called "literary club" whose reading matter was more apt to be political tracts than *belles lettres*. Among its members were a cavalry officer, a few minor government officials, a grocer and a postal clerk — discontented *criollos* all. By the summer of 1810 they were plotting an armed uprising for December. But the plot was uncovered in early September, and several of the conspirators were arrested.

Word reached Hidalgo on the night of September 15 that royalist authorities were heading for his village with orders to arrest him. So, early on the next morning, a Sunday, Hidalgo rang the church bells to summon his parishioners — but not to mass. Instead he bade them strike for independence immediately. "A new dispensation comes to us today," he cried. "Will you recover the lands stolen 300 years ago from your forefathers by the hated Spaniards? We must act at once," he went on. "Death to bad government! Death to the *gachupines!*"

Hidalgo's Indian parishioners responded with a fervor that no one had anticipated. They swiftly armed themselves with sticks, machetes and shovels, and with Hidalgo in the lead they set off to meet the royalists head on.

Hidalgo was a well-meaning idealist who had no training as a commander, and he was quite unable to control the conflagration he had started. His impromptu army was joined on the march by recruits from the haciendas and the mines, and it coalesced into a mob bent on sheer destruction. They went rampaging through town after town, and they massacred soldiers and civilians alike. In the town of Guanajuato alone, 2,500 people perished.

By late October, Hidalgo's unruly force had swollen to 80,000 and was marching toward the royalist army stronghold in Mexico City.

Then Hidalgo hesitated. He seems to have fretted over the death and destruction his followers had already caused, and to have feared what might lie ahead in the capital. At any rate, he withdrew his army to the northwest. While he contemplated his next move, the mob began to disintegrate. Hidalgo was captured and executed. The royalists, determined to give a grisly warning to any future insurgents, fastened his head to a pole and exhibited it on a charred wall in Guanajuato, the site of his first big victory.

The torch of rebellion was picked up by one of Hidalgo's fellow conspirators, José María Morelos. Like Hidalgo, Morelos was a village priest, but he also proved to be a practical man and a better tactician — both politically and on the battlefield. He organized and trained a small army in guerrilla tactics and by 1813 succeeded in cutting Mexico City's communications with both coasts. Meanwhile, he had formulated a truly revolutionary vision of a caste-free republic with all lands restored to the Indians. He then summoned a congress in Chilpancingo, in the western mountains, to issue a declaration of independence and a constitution.

Those *criollos* who had not been repelled by all the bloodshed were now dismayed by the unexpected turn the movement was taking. *Criollos* wanted a chance to rule their affairs independently of Spain, but they had no desire

found their instrument in Agustín de Iturbide, a cunning and ambitious *criollo* who as a colonel in the royalist army had been fighting the insurgents on and off for more than a decade.

Sent by the viceroy with 2,500 troops to crush an uprising in Oaxaca, Iturbide saw an opportunity to seize power. He switched allegiance. He made a deal with the guerrilla chieftain Vicente Guerrero to put all the troops in his command at the service of independence, in exchange for the right to dictate the terms of independence. He wanted Mexico organized as a constitutional monarchy; the Roman Catholic religion to be the official religion of the country; *criollos* and *peninsulares* to be treated equally in the new state; and a new army, the Ejército de las Tres Garantías (the Army of the Three Guarantees), to be placed under his command.

Iturbide got his way, and with practically no opposition he marched into Mexico City on September 27, 1821, declaring himself head of a new and independent government. The colony was now the sovereign state of Mexico — a name taken from a word the Aztecs used to describe themselves.

Liberation from Spain had cost Mexico dearly. Some estimates put the toll as high as 600,000 lives in 11 years of rebellion. But the bloodshed brought little change in the social structure. The *peninsulares* departed for home, taking with them whatever silver bullion they could carry and leaving the state treasury empty. And in the meantime, rich *criollos* got richer by seizing land abandoned by the *peninsulares*. The church retained its privileges of exemption from taxation and from trial in civil courts.

Iturbide proclaimed Mexico an empire and installed himself as Emperor

for a social revolution that would deprive them of land, wealth or privilege. Morelos lost their support. But he made a resounding appeal to *mestizos*, invoking the hallowed name of the emperor Moctezuma and calling on his fellow *mestizos* to avenge the enslavement of the last three centuries.

While the delegates whom Morelos had convened at Chilpancingo dickered over the terms of a constitution, the royalist army broke out of Mexico City and in brutal fighting went on to reclaim the other cities that had fallen to the rebels — including Chilpancingo. The constitution died a-borning, and Morelos had to flee to the countryside. A year and a half later, in the autumn of 1815, the army caught up with him, tried him for treason and executed him before a firing squad in Mexico City.

For the next five years the independence movement went leaderless, sputtering on in the form of intermittent but bloody insurrection and vicious guerrilla raids here and there. Then in 1821, when there seemed little reason to expect it, independence was finally achieved — though hardly in the manner envisioned by the two priests who had sacrificed their lives.

The climate among *criollos* had now swung back in favor of independence — partly because with the passage of time they had forgotten the savagery of the early battles, and partly because the status quo in the mother country had changed. Napoleon's designs on Spain had long since failed, and now the Spanish nobles were pressing demands for constitutional reform upon their current monarch, Ferdinand VII. Any democratic advances made in Spain were likely to benefit the colonials. In any event, the *criollos* reasoned, the time to renew the cause of independence was when the king was beset from another quarter. They

A CHRONOLOGY OF KEY EVENTS

c. 20,000 B.C. Early hunters appear in Mexico's Central Valley. These Paleo-Indians — descendants of migrants who had come to the New World via the Bering Strait land bridge — used crudely shaped weapons to kill game.

c. 5000 B.C. Farming begins in Mexico.

c. 1500 B.C. Villages are established, simple trade begins and artists create ceramics both useful and beautiful.

900-400 B.C. Olmec civilization reaches its height in the sweltering Gulf Coast region of southern Veracruz and neighboring Tabasco. Olmec sculptors carve realistic stone heads *(below)*, impressive ceremonial centers are built, and writing begins in Mexico.

c. 200 B.C. Teotihuacán — whose origins remain a mystery — emerges as the cultural and political heart of the Central Valley. Its immense urban complex eventually encompasses a group of great temple pyramids adorned with frescoes and sculpture.

600-900 A.D. Mayan culture, which dominated southeastern Mexico and much of Central America, enters its great age of expansion and brilliance, producing majestic buildings, murals, bas-reliefs and a calendar.

c. 900 Northern warriors known as Toltecs conquer the Central Valley under the powerful leader Mixcóatl. His son, Topiltzin, becomes high priest of a cult honoring Quetzalcóatl, the god believed to have created the human race from his own blood. Topiltzin founds the city of Tula in about 968 and controls most of Central Mexico.

987 Following a struggle between his sect and adherents of Tezcatlipoca, the bloody ancestral deity of the Toltecs, Topiltzin and his partisans migrate to the Yucatán Peninsula, where they merge with the Mayan civilization.

1168-1179 The Toltec capital of Tula falls to a new wave of northern warriors, the Chichimecs.

1345 The Aztecs, last of the Chichimecs, found Tenochtitlán, guided there by the sight of an eagle-like bird perched on a cactus *(below)*, fulfilling their god Huitzilopochtli's prophecy.

1427 Itzcóatl becomes ruler of the Aztecs. He founds the empire that is later to dazzle the Spanish conquerors under Hernán Cortés *(below)*.

1519 The Aztec ruler Moctezuma II yields to the Spaniards, opening the door to the destruction of the Aztec empire in 1521.

1523 The first Spanish monks begin missionary work that is destined to convert millions of Indians to Christianity by the end of the century.

1531 An Aztec convert brings word of a vision of a dark-skinned Virgin Mary to a bishop, who builds a shrine in the town of Guadalupe. The Indians take the Virgin's appearance as a blessing, and the veneration of the Virgin of Guadalupe becomes a unifying factor in Mexican Catholicism.

1535 Don Antonio de Mendoza arrives in New Spain as first viceroy. By 1550 the colonial government is on firm footing, politically stable and economically healthy.

1767 The Jesuits are ordered to leave Mexico by Spain's King Charles III, who feels threatened by their political activities.

1810 Father Miguel Hidalgo y Costilla leads an uprising of Indians and *mestizos*, beginning 11 years of wars for independence from Spain.

1821 Mexican independence is achieved when the captain general of New Spain signs a treaty with insurgents who are led by Colonel Agustín de Iturbide.

1822 Iturbide declares himself emperor of Mexico and begins a strife-torn reign of less than seven months.

1824 The 19 states and four territories of Mexico are organized into a federal republic.

1829 Spanish troops attempt to retake Mexico but are repelled by forces commanded by General Antonio López de Santa Anna *(below)*.

1833 Santa Anna is elected president and begins an erratic political career that is to see him in and out of office 11 times in the next 20 years.

1846-1848 Mexico fights a war with the United States and loses. In signing the Treaty of Guadalupe-Hidalgo, it cedes more than half its territory to the U.S., including Texas, New Mexico and Northern California.

1857 A new constitution, providing for a unicameral legislature and Mexico's first genuine bill of rights, takes effect.

1858-1861 Benito Juárez *(below)*, a Zapotec Indian, promulgates laws separating church and state. He leads liber-

al forces in a three-year war of reform against conservatives, which ends with his election as president.

1861 Spanish, British and French troops occupy Veracruz in an attempt to collect debts — some of them half a century old — that are owed to their countries by Mexico. The Spanish and British forces withdraw; the French troops march inland.

1863 The French seize control of the country. Napoleon III installs Ferdinand Maximilian Josef of Austria as Emperor Maximilian of Mexico.

1867 Benito Juárez retakes the government; Emperor Maximilian is executed by a firing squad. An era of restoration begins.

1876 Porfirio Díaz becomes president and begins a 35-year tenure that stabilizes the country and bolsters its image abroad.

1884 The Mexican government allows foreign companies to prospect for oil. Systematic geological exploration begins after 1900, leading to commercial oil production by American and British investors.

1910 The Mexican revolution begins and President Díaz is overthrown. This is the start of a 10-year period of civil war, in which angry peasant masses and frustrated middle-class reformists fight the conservatives and one another for political hegemony.

1914 Emiliano Zapata, leader of agrarian forces in the south, and Pancho Villa, chief of the northern rebels, form a short-lived alliance to chase Venustiano Carranza, head of the provisional government, from Mexico City. During the course of the revolution, insurgent armies occupy Mexico City five times.

1915 In the battle of Celaya, the most famous military engagement of the Mexican revolution, rebels led by Pancho Villa twice take the offensive against the Constitutionalist forces commanded by Alvaro Obregón and suffer staggering losses.

1917 A new constitution provides for free and compulsory education and sets forth requirements for land and labor reform; it also limits church power and curbs foreign investments.

1918 Labor leader Luis Morones founds Mexico's first union.

1920 Alvaro Obregón becomes president and sets about reconstructing the country. Thousands of new schools and libraries are built; redistribution of land begins in rural areas, and union membership rises dramatically in towns and cities.

1926 In response to governmental moves against the church, the Mexican archbishop calls a strike by the clergy. During the resulting Cristero rebellion, clashes break out between Catholic guerrillas and government troops.

1929 Plutarco Elías Calles establishes an official national political party, the Partido Nacional Revolucionario (PNR), later renamed the Partido Revolucionario Institucional (PRI).

1934 Lázaro Cárdenas becomes president and makes good on the promises of the revolution, distributing 50 million acres of land among the peasants over the next six years.

1938 President Cárdenas nationalizes the petroleum industry.

1942 Mexico enters World War II on the side of the Allies.

1946-1952 Miguel Alemán, Mexico's first civilian president in 35 years, allows the agrarian revolution to languish as the nation embarks on a period of rapid economic growth. Alemán sponsors public-works projects, in-

cluding construction of dams, highways, hydroelectric stations and an improved communications network.

1955 The full enfranchisement of women marks the culmination of years of active campaigning by women's organizations throughout the country.

1968 Olympic Summer Games *(above)* are held in Mexico City; to show itself a proper host, the nation spends between $150 million and $200 million for the construction of athletic facilities, hotels and a subway system.

1972 Government-sponsored birth-control clinics begin a campaign to slow population growth; the birth rate falls nearly half a percent in a decade.

1981 Oil becomes Mexico's principal export after production *(below)* quadruples in less than 10 years.

1982 Severe inflation sets in, prompting devaluations of the peso. President de la Madrid outlines a plan for economic recovery, based on limiting foreign borrowing, reducing government spending and restricting imports.

1985 Economic problems persist. De la Madrid imposes new austerity measures, but his administration loses political credit.

4

Agustín I. His reign was brief; he was overthrown in less than seven months, and the empire was abolished. But he ushered in a chaotic era. Struggle followed struggle between liberals and conservatives, between republicans and monarchists, between federalists and centralists, between anticlericals and proponents of clerical privilege. Because army men had brought about independence, army men were to play the most conspicuous role in Mexican government for the next century. During the following 30 years, one military dictator, or *caudillo,* after another would set himself up as president, then call for a pro forma election to make his title official — only to be removed by another who did the same. In coup and countercoup, the government changed hands more than 40 times.

In that bewildering period, Mexico lost more than half its land; Texas asserted its independence, and the Territories of Arizona, New Mexico and California were relinquished to the United States for piecemeal sums that totaled little more than $28 million. Not until 1857 did Mexico acquire a constitution that would lay the groundwork for political stability, and a leader to make it stick. He was Benito Juárez.

Juárez — a full-blooded Zapotec Indian — was by any measure an extraordinary figure. He had been orphaned at the age of three and might have lived out his life as a laborer on a *criollo*-owned hacienda. But when he was 12, he went to work as houseboy for a Franciscan lay brother who took an interest in him. He learned to read, attended school with the priest's help, and went on to study law and enter politics.

By 1856 Juárez had become minister of justice in Mexico City under a more or less liberal *caudillo.* He helped draft the constitution of 1857, which called for a legislature to be elected by representatives of the municipalities, and a president to be elected for a specified term by the legislature. The constitution abolished all titles of nobility and, for the first time in Mexican history, provided a bill of rights, guaranteeing freedom of speech and assembly. It also made clerics and soldiers subject to trial in civil courts, and required that all church lands except those devoted specifically to religious worship be seized by the government and turned over to the Indians.

For the next several decades, however, the constitution was honored mainly in the breach. Few influential Mexicans were ready for such liberal legislation, and the conservatives' hostile reactions brought three more years of civil strife, beginning in 1857, when a conservative coup forced the liberal government from Mexico City. Ousted from the capital, the liberals still refused to surrender; they named Juárez president. But the conservatives raised an army and chased Juárez and the liberals north. He moved from one temporary capital to another in a plain black carriage. Not until 1861 did liberal victories on the battlefield enable him to return to Mexico City.

Almost immediately, Juárez was faced with another threat — foreign intervention. Constant warfare and graft and mismanagement by his predecessors had emptied the treasury; when Juárez took over, the army, the civil servants and the police had not been paid for months. Juárez therefore declared a two-year moratorium on the payment of all foreign debts, including compensation for French and British property destroyed in the fighting.

Angered over the stoppage of pay-ments, Emperor Napoleon III of France used it as a pretext for gaining a foothold in the New World. French troops landed at Veracruz and drove Juárez' government back into northern exile. Mexican conservatives saw this as an opportunity to reassert their privileged status, and conspired to turn Mexico into a French puppet state. The man they chose for the purpose was an Austrian archduke, Ferdinand Maximilian Josef, then 30 years old.

The archduke was a younger brother of Emperor Franz Josef of Austria and had no expectation of gaining the throne in his homeland. As a Hapsburg and thus a distant kinsman to the Spanish royal house, Maximilian was suitable to Mexican conservatives — and to Napoleon III, who thought it wise to have the Austrians on his side. In addition, all parties to the bargain considered Maximilian unintelligent and easy to manipulate.

Maximilian arrived in a style befitting his title. He rode around Mexico City with his young wife, Carlota, in an ornate coach and established a regal court in Chapultepec Castle. Such flaunting of extravagance could hardly appeal to the downtrodden Mexicans. Yet, to the surprise and dismay of the conservatives who had put him in power, Maximilian proved to have some distinctly liberal tendencies. He encouraged a free press and pardoned political prisoners. When a papal nuncio came from Rome with the demand that property seized from the church by the terms of the 1857 constitution be restored, Maximilian astonished the world by refusing to cooperate.

In doing this he succeeded in antagonizing the very conservatives who had helped to put him in power, but at the same time he failed to win over the lib-

Indian and *mestizo* laborers toil to remove silver ore from a mine in the 1890s. Miners like these worked under such hardships and discriminatory treatment that their unrest would help ignite the 1910 revolution.

erals, who were too bent on overthrowing this foreign interloper to give him credit for anything.

Meanwhile, the French army that was to have been the backbone of Maximilian's regime was finding Mexico and the Mexicans most intractable. The first forces that landed in January 1862 had now been built up to 7,000 men, but they had only a tenuous hold on the country and were harassed by guerrillas everywhere. Worse yet, in May the French suffered a sharp defeat at Puebla, a textile-manufacturing city on the sandy plains about 65 miles southeast of Mexico City.

From his headquarters in the north, Juárez had managed to rally 5,000 troops, and he sent them south to Puebla, where they laid a trap for the French. When the French cavalry tried to charge Puebla's defenses, the Mexicans, concealed behind tall cactus plants, threw the French into a state of disarray. The French used up half their ammunition in two hours of confused fighting and were finally put to flight. The hero of the day was a young brigadier general by the name of Porfirio Díaz, who was later to parlay his way into politics on the basis of it.

Meanwhile Napoleon III was having doubts about the venture. The United States had let his government know that the French presence south of the border was unwelcome by supplying arms to Juárez and sending a 100,000-man army to the banks of the Rio Grande. Alarmed by this and threatened at home by Prussian advances on France, Napoleon III began withdrawing his army in 1866. Maximilian's posi-

4

tion became untenable. The following year the liberals crushed the few remaining French troops and executed the would-be emperor himself.

In stark contrast to the showy extravagance of Maximilian, Juárez returned to Mexico City on July 15, 1867, riding in the plain black carriage that had served as his movable office for four years. Crowds lined the streets waving placards and strewing garlands. Porfirio Díaz, the general who had driven the French out of Puebla, was on hand to present the national flag to Juárez, who ran it up the flagpole, exclaiming: *"Viva México!"* The crowd responded with a roar. "The people and the government shall respect the rights of all," he told his eager audience. He vowed to make Mexico a land of laws.

But that was to prove no easy chore. Among other things, Juárez instituted education that was compulsory, free and independent of the church, and for this he was assailed as being antireligious. He demobilized the army— only to discover that the men he had turned out into the countryside soon became bandits. Yet he retained the love of his countrymen. He won reelection twice and died in office of a heart attack in 1872, having presided over his country for nearly 15 years.

The presidency passed to Juárez' hand-picked successor, Sebastián Lerdo de Tejado, who was chief justice. But Lerdo's mind for legal niceties did not serve him as president. In 1876, before he had completed his term, he was overthrown in a military coup led by Porfirio Díaz.

Díaz was of part Indian ancestry and, like Juárez, a native of the state of Oaxaca. He had also studied law, but he lacked the old leader's almost mystical faith in the law. Having seized the presidency by force, he held it — for three decades — by force and cunning. He placated the church by ignoring the reforms of the liberal constitution and allowing religious schools to reappear. Instead of ignoring the army, as Juárez had done, he mobilized it anew and rewarded his generals with permanent commands; but he shrewdly scattered them in remote parts of the land to prevent their banding together in a coup against him.

Díaz made the legislature so subservient that he could call its members *"mi caballada"* — "my herd of tame horses." He curbed the press by imprisoning — and in some instances assassinating — newspapermen who disagreed with him. Finally, to control the bandits who roamed the provinces — and at the same time provide a counterpoise to the army — he built up a fierce national police force, the *rurales*.

His strong-arm tactics had a positive aspect, however, for the 55 years of upheaval prior to his coming had left the nation exhausted, its treasury nearly empty. Díaz brought peace to the countryside, order to the nation's chaotic finances and life to its inert industries. He balanced the budget and paid off much of the foreign debt, then gave special tax exemptions to encourage foreign investors to put their money in Mexico. They did; by 1910 foreign investments totaled more than $1.3 billion. And with foreign money came foreign technological know-how.

When Díaz first took office in 1876, Mexico had no more than 400 miles of railroad track, and that scant trackage ran only between Mexico City and Veracruz. Goods being hauled overland anywhere else in the country had to go by mule train or ox-drawn wagon — a slow and tortuous undertaking in any land, but more so in Mexico, with its mountains and ravines. By the time he left office in 1911, Mexican railroads — with the help of foreigners — had been extended to 15,000 miles.

The railroads made possible a quantum leap in industrialization. Silver production increased fourfold; cotton textile production trebled; other resources that Mexico had never tapped before — among them, lead, zinc and oil — began to be developed. New industries sprang up; steel and copper were produced. All told, the volume of manufactured goods doubled.

The benefits, however, went chiefly to the well-to-do — the foreign investors and the *criollos*. Furthering themselves even more, the *criollos* used the land laws passed by the Díaz legislature of "tame horses" to extend their already considerable holdings.

One new law of 1883 called for a survey of national lands. Anyone could obtain a government contract for surveying, and as payment help himself to one third of the land surveyed. The other two thirds would remain with the government, which under the same law could sell the lands at bargain prices in blocks of up to 6,000 acres. Within nine years a staggering 134.5 million acres of public land went to personal friends of Díaz and to foreigners. All told, one fifth of Mexico's entire land mass passed into the hands of a few hundred wealthy families between 1883 and 1894. One family owned more than 50 ranches, totaling seven million acres, on which grazed 500,000 head of cattle, 225,000 sheep and 25,000 horses.

Already more than half of the rural population lived in peonage on the great haciendas. By the end of the Díaz regime fewer than 10 percent of the Indians would own land. They were

perpetually in debt, and they were bound by law to remain on the estates so long as they owed a single *centavo* to the *hacendado,* the owner.

The Indians consigned to industrial and mining labor were no better off; they toiled 12 hours a day, seven days a week. If they tried to better their conditions by organizing strikes, they risked being gunned down by the *rurales* or by army troops. Not surprisingly, resentment smoldered beneath the surface, yet Porfirio Díaz ruled on uncontested. In fact, he ruled so long that people began to refer to him as Don Perpetuo and wondered if he would live and govern forever. In 1908, however, when he was 78 years old, he told an American journalist that he meant to retire from the presidency when his term ended in 1910, two years hence.

A few Mexicans took the old dictator at his word, most notably a *criollo* rancher named Francisco Indalecio Madero, who was a member of one of Mexico's wealthiest families. Madero was unusual in that he showed a keen interest in the welfare of his workers, accepting from scribes among them written complaints of injustices, which he then tried to rectify. He also dabbled in spiritualism, and it is said that when a Ouija board once told him that he was destined to be president, he believed it. He was at work on a book called *The Presidential Succession in 1910* when he heard that Díaz was talking of retirement.

His book turned out to be a modest one, proposing nothing more radical than that political parties organize to elect a vice president to succeed Díaz, and that the presidential tenure be limited to a single term. But when published in early 1909, the book sparked so much public interest that Madero was hailed as the "apostle of democracy" and was catapulted into the campaign for the presidency himself. His opponent was Díaz, who ran again after all. When Díaz saw that Madero was attracting large and enthusiastic crowds, he threw him in jail on a trumped-up charge of fomenting rebellion.

Madero managed to escape and, disguised as a railroad laborer, retreated north to San Antonio, Texas. There he proclaimed himself provisional president and called for the Mexican people to take up arms against the Díaz regime. He set the time and date for 6 p.m. on Sunday, November 20, 1910.

The people responded with a vengeance. And thus, quite unexpectedly, was launched the Mexican revolution — the bloodiest and most confused of the wars in a nation already noted for death and disorder. Citizens of all kinds joined the revolution: barefoot Indians in serapes and middle-class shopkeepers in business suits; ranchers with high-crowned sombreros and old bandits with bandoliers strapped across their chests; reformers like Madero who merely wanted to restore democracy and radicals who wanted to sweep away the old order altogether. In background, education, occupation, income and social class, and even in their goals,

they were as heterogeneous a group as ever took up arms. But they were united in opposition to Díaz and in the belief that Mexico was due for change and emergence into the modern world.

The rebels had no plan, no training and only meager funds. They lived off the land and learned guerrilla tactics as they fought — and they fought a savage war. They killed, burned, looted and raped; any prisoners they took were usually executed.

Typical of their virulence was the action of a general in the state of Chihuahua. After his men had ambushed and destroyed a large federal convoy, he had the enemy dead stripped and their uniforms bundled together and sent off to Mexico City. Attached was a note for Díaz: "Here are the wrappers; send me some more tamales."

Díaz' army, which was led by men as elderly as himself, was no match for the ragtag bands of rebels — and neither was the once invincible dictator. Scarcely six months after the start of the revolution, he resigned and fled the capital. "Madero has unleashed a tiger," Díaz said bitterly en route to the port of Veracruz and thence to European exile. "Now let's see if he can control it."

Madero had certainly set events in motion, and there were signs that his control was shaky. The motley group of men who had answered his call already was rent by personal and ideological rivalries, and his arrival in Mexico City was heralded by an earthquake that cracked walls and shattered the train platform on which he was to alight — bad omens to a superstitious man.

During 16 months in office, Madero faced six different major rebellions from the left and the right. One was led by Félix Díaz, nephew of the deposed dictator. To put down Díaz and his insurgents, Madero assigned General Victoriano Huerta. The general was a broad-shouldered, hard-drinking *mestizo* who ran a chain of gambling houses and reaped additional profit from the army by arranging to have one son handle arms and ammunition contracts and another deal in military uniforms.

As treacherous as he was rapacious, Huerta quickly turned on President Madero, ordered him arrested and seized the presidency. Three days later the would-be "apostle of democracy" was gunned down by the *rurales,* ostensibly while attempting to escape.

The Huerta regime was even more brutal than that of Díaz. The general dissolved Congress and arrested most of its members. He closed the courts and embarked upon a wave of political assassinations remarkable for their crudity. Within 10 days of assuming the presidency, he had 100 supporters of Madero machine-gunned, and he disposed of the liberal governor of rebellious Chihuahua by having him hurled under the wheels of a moving train.

His actions only provoked a new wave of fury — and brought a new cast of characters onstage. Soon Mexico was aflame with sundry rebels led by three of the fiercest and ablest commanders who ever waged guerrilla warfare — Emiliano Zapata, Pancho Villa and Alvaro Obregón. Their goals were not spelled out in detail, but they had a common slogan, *Tierra y libertad!* — Land and liberty! — and for a decade it would be heard all across the country as they attempted to change the social order.

In the south, marauding through his home state of Morelos, was Emiliano Zapata, a slender, dark-skinned, well-muscled farmer and former rodeo trick rider. Zapata was the most selfless and single-minded of the revolutionary chieftains; he was a true champion of

the Indians and their claim to land.

Proudly wearing the white pants and white shirts that identified them as field laborers, and shouting "Land and liberty!" the Zapatistas swooped down on hacienda after hacienda. When a hacienda surrendered, Zapata would expropriate it and divide up the land among the peasants who had been working it. Whenever a hacienda held out, his ferocity knew no bounds. Once inside, his men would lay waste the whole estate, burning buildings and crops to the ground.

In the northern state of Chihuahua, Zapata had his counterpart in Pancho Villa. The son of a poor sharecropper, Villa became a bandit at the age of 16 and set out to establish himself as a sort of Robin Hood among the Indians.

"God brought me into the world to battle," Villa once told a journalist, and indeed he made fighting a lifetime career. The tricks of the outlaw's trade served him well in the revolution. His rebels hijacked federal army trains and stole cattle, then sold the animals across the border in New Mexico to buy arms. He built his Division of the North into a superb guerrilla army complete with artillery and even its own hospital train to care for the wounded.

To the west, in the state of Sonora, the rebels were led by Alvaro Obregón, a *criollo* who had become disgusted by the excesses of his class. A mechanic and small farmer who had invented a machine for picking *garbanzos,* or chickpeas, he was municipal president of the town of Huatabampo and a relative newcomer to the revolution. Initially the Indians under his command were armed with nothing more sophisticated than bows and arrows, but Obregón remedied that in short order by capturing huge quantities of artillery, guns, ammunition and other stores from federal troops.

In the struggle against Huerta, both Obregón and Villa answered to a more imposing (if less popular) rebel than themselves — Venustiano Carranza, the governor of the state of Coahuila. In some respects, Carranza was an anomaly among revolutionaries. He came from a family of wealthy landowners and thus had an air of patrician respectability. He also had elegant tastes; he enjoyed good food and traveled in his own private three-car train.

Carranza was a politician rather than a soldier, and he wanted to restore the old Juárez constitution of 1857. He managed to persuade Villa and Obre-

111

4

gón to join him in a loose military alliance known as the Constitutionalists. Carranza planned to assume the presidency himself if the revolt against Huerta succeeded.

By 1913, when Carranza joined the fray, the revolution had become so heated that virtually the entire country was involved. Conspicuous among the forces now were the *soldaderas,* women who followed the men of every army off to war, often with infants slung on their backs. They foraged for provisions, cooked, did the laundry and nursed the wounded. So important did the *soldaderas* become that when the Huerta government proposed to ban them from federal campaigns, the men of one battalion threatened to mutiny. The women remained.

Faced with well-led, well-equipped and determined rebel armies in the north, the south and the west, Huerta's forces absorbed defeat after defeat and were sent into retreat on all fronts. Meanwhile, his regime was suffering economically as well. The mines shut down, and the crops went unharvested. The federal treasury was bankrupt, and rebel armies, states and private banks took to printing their own paper money; late in 1913 at least 25 different worthless currencies were circulating. The only faction to turn out a currency of any value was the supposedly unsophisticated peasant army of Zapata. They cast their coins from melted-down bars of solid silver.

A severe blow to the government came in April 1914, when the U.S. government — concerned about the security of the oil wells in which Americans had invested — sent gunboats to blockade Veracruz, the major port on the Gulf Coast. This action cut off the Huerta government's customs duties, a vital source of revenue, and interrupted the delivery of 200 machine guns and 15 million rounds of ammunition aboard a German vessel. The ship sailed south and landed her cargo farther down the coast, but the Huerta regime could ill afford the delay.

By now the rebel armies were scoring further gains everywhere. In June 1914, at the north-central mining town of Zacatecas, Villa threw 23,000 rebels against 12,000 federals; only a few hundred escaped. Villa's stunning victory was soon followed by another, the capture of Guadalajara by Obregón. Those two battles sealed Huerta's fate. On August 14, 1914, Obregón's rebels moved into Mexico City and claimed the capital for Carranza, as Huerta followed Díaz into exile.

The victors had no sooner seized the government than they fell to squabbling over personal and ideological differences that would cause the fighting to rage on for five more tumultuous years. Carranza sensed a political rival in Villa and cut off the latter's coal supply, thus immobilizing locomotives that Villa was counting on to move his men south — and enabling Obregón to beat Villa into Mexico City. That turn of events so angered Villa that he joined with Zapata to drive Carranza from Mexico City. As they neared the capital, Carranza withdrew his provisional government to Veracruz. The two revolutionaries entered the capital in triumph, but then Zapata lost interest in Villa's concern with Mexico City; he pulled out his men and led them home to Morelos and the fields they had won.

In the years since 1910, the revolution had developed a terrible momentum. Many Mexicans no longer knew what they were fighting for, so much had blood lust become a way of life. "It

At the head of his fierce guerrilla force, Pancho Villa gallops into Torreón after taking the city in 1913. As a result of the day-long battle, the untutored Villa won a reputation for being a brilliant military tactician.

4

is good fighting," a former miner named Juan Sánchez told an American journalist. "You don't have to work in the mines."

For a time, no fewer than four different governments claimed to represent Mexico. Carranza was the most durable and the most widely recognized of the pretenders to office, but he was forced to conduct the business of government from Veracruz so long as Villa continued to hold Mexico City.

Meanwhile, the bloodletting went on. The decisive battles were waged between Villa and Obregón, who was still fighting in the name of Carranza and the so-called Constitutionalist army. Early in 1915, Obregón drove Villa from Mexico City and pursued him north as far as the state of Guanajuato.

Obregón had been studying the tactics employed in the war then being waged in France, and he adopted them for himself. He occupied the city of Celaya, and entrenched his men behind coils of barbed wire and batteries of machine guns. When Villa counterattacked, wave after wave of men and horses rushed up to the barbed-wire defenses, and there they died. In just two battles only a week apart in April 1915, Villa lost at least 6,000 men, a quarter of his army, and possibly more than twice that. Villa was squeezed northward into the mountains of Chihuahua and was soon reduced to leading a mere band of outlaws.

With Villa on the run and Zapata's rebels planting their fields in Morelos, presidential pretender Carranza slowly gained the upper hand. His government won official recognition from the United States in October 1915. This so infuriated Villa, who had cultivated American friendship and been treated as a hero in American newspapers, that

he went on a rampage. His men stopped a train and murdered 16 American mining engineers and technicians and then raided and terrorized the New Mexico border town of Columbus, killing another 18 Americans. The U.S. responded by sending General John Pershing and 6,000 troops on an expedition to catch Villa. But Villa was far too wily to be captured easily; he now vanished into the hills.

By 1917, Carranza was again established in Mexico City, and under his leadership a new constitution was ratified. It articulated the aims of the revolution, giving coherence to the often-inchoate goals of the people who waged it and laying the foundations for modern Mexico. It firmly separated church and state (putting education under the aegis of the state and forbidding clergymen to hold office), and recognized the rights of laborers to organize unions. It also declared that all natural resources such as oil and minerals belonged to the nation as a whole and — most sweeping — it empowered the government to redistribute land to the peasants who had been yearning for it so long.

But by 1917, when the constitution was adopted, there was little revolutionary idealism left. Carranza himself alienated most of the old revolutionaries; his administration was conservative, corrupt and inert. When confronted with a crisis, he would stare through blue-tinted spectacles and thoughtfully comb the fingers of his left hand through his long white beard. Obregón observed tartly to a friend that Carranza was "a great man for little things and a small man for great ones."

Zapata, who was still preoccupied with the Indians and their land in Morelos, had a harsher indictment. He summed up his resentment in an open

letter addressed to "Citizen Carranza" in March of 1919.

"You turned the struggle to your own advantage and that of your friends who helped your rise and then shared the booty — riches, businesses, banquets, sumptuous feasts, bacchanals, orgies," Zapata wrote. "It never occurred to you that the revolution was fought to benefit the great masses, the legions of the oppressed whom you motivated by your harangues."

Carranza's response was a complicated and successful plot to draw Zapata into a trap. Deceiving Zapata with a fake offer of troops and support from a federal general, he lured him into a meeting with the supposed turncoat at a hacienda in Zapata's territory. As Zapata reached the threshold of the door, one of the troops recalled, "at point blank, without giving him time even to draw his pistols, the soldiers who were presenting arms fired two volleys, and our unforgettable General Zapata fell, never to rise again." He was 39.

Carranza himself had not long to govern. Though Obregón was his logical successor, Carranza chose another candidate for the 1920 presidential elections. The outraged Obregón organized yet another rebellion. In May 1920 his new army was marching toward the capital. Carranza, following the time-honored path of fallen presidents, fled toward Veracruz. En route he stopped to rest in a village in Puebla, and there he was assassinated in bed by one of his former comrades.

Villa survived for a while. Obregón and his supporters were determined to have peace and, to get Villa to lay down his arms, made a deal with him. In what must be the deepest irony of that confused and ironical time, the lifelong bandit became the proprietor of a

Alvaro Obregón, leader of the Constitutionalist forces, lost his right arm battling Villa's troops in 1915. Severely wounded by a shell, he found the pain so excruciating that he tried to shoot himself, but his pistol was unloaded. After amputation, his shattered arm was preserved in alcohol and ended up as a relic, housed in a monument to Obregón in Mexico City.

25,000-acre hacienda in his home state of Durango. He was not fated to live happily ever after, however; in July 1923, having enjoyed only three years as a gentleman farmer, he was ambushed in his car by a gang of assassins, who pumped 47 bullets into his body. They were never identified, much less caught, but presumably they were bandits who felt he had betrayed them.

Meanwhile, Alvaro Obregón hoped to legitimize his takeover by calling for an election. He was duly elected, and his inauguration in 1920 put an end at long last to the feudalism imposed by the Spanish conquerors four centuries before. The cost of the 10-year revolution had been almost incalculable. Most of the country lay in ruins, and one in every eight Mexicans had died — two million in all. Obregón, who had lost his right arm in battle, brought to the awesome task of reconstruction a grim sense of humor. "All of us are thieves, more or less," he said. "However, I have only one hand, while the others have two. That is why people prefer me."

Obregón also came to office with a determination to maintain the peace, a willingness to compromise and a desire to rebuild on the ruins of the old order by implementing the constitution of 1917, which had been largely ignored by Carranza. But to put the constitution into effect was a large order that would take many years. Obregón made a modest start. He began distributing land in *ejidos,* the communal parcels that represented a return to an ancient Indian practice. Obregón's most important accomplishment, however, was to make possible an orderly transfer of power. When his elected successor took office in 1924, the presidency changed hands peacefully for the first time in 40 years.

The vestigial violence of the revolution caught up with Obregón in 1928. He sought the presidency again, and only 17 days after his reelection he was assassinated by a young religious fanatic. In the wake of Obregón's death came a new mechanism for stability — the Partido Nacional Revolucionario, the National Revolutionary Party, founded in 1929 and made up of the various revolutionary factions. The party gave Mexico its first real opportunity for a peaceful transfer of political power by providing for open political campaigns and duly convoked conventions where personal and ideological struggles could be resolved by discussion and ballot instead of bloodshed.

Obregón, Madero, Zapata, Carranza, Villa — all of the great revolutionary leaders had died violently, but the ideals for which they fought lived on. One by one, the goals of the revolution began to be reached through words and law instead of weapons.

The revolution had not ended poverty and illiteracy. But it had brought political stability, economic progress and a measure of social justice rare in the world's developing countries.

It had also forged a nation. When Díaz took over in 1876, and even as late as 1910, at the outset of the revolution, Mexico was not truly a nation, but a mix of diverse groups who happened to reside within the same geographical borders. The revolution, for all its griefs, terrors and cruel ironies, produced a people who despite vast differences of wealth have managed to put aside age-old and deep-rooted prejudices of caste and come to share a sense of national unity and uniqueness. And out of the revolution came a great flowering of art, architecture and literature giving expression to that nationhood. □

ZAPATA AND HIS ARMY IN WHITE

Of all the leaders in the revolution, Emiliano Zapata was the most idealistic. He sought neither personal power nor wealth. His one goal was to restore to the peasants of his native state of Morelos "the lands, woods and water that the landlords or bosses have usurped from us." To the Indians of Morelos, land was more important than life itself. They spoke feelingly of their *patria chica* (little fatherland), and the song they loved best ended with the refrain: "If they are going to kill me tomorrow, / Why, let them kill me today."

Zapata had hated the landlords ever since childhood, when hacienda guards beat him for taking hay from hacienda land — hay that was to have been burned anyway. In 1910 he helped form the landless peasants into a disciplined guerrilla army. Shouting their slogan, *Tierra y libertad* (land and liberty), Zapatistas waged hit-and-run war on federal troops and seized the land of rich hacienda owners to give it to the peasants.

Zapata never saw his dream of land reform realized. Lured into a trap by federal soldiers in 1919, a year before the revolution ended, he was cold-bloodedly gunned down. He was only 39, and many Morelos Indians refused to believe he was dead. On dark nights, they said, he could still be seen upon his white horse, patrolling the hills.

Though slight in stature, Zapata, who usually wore peasant garb, was an impressive figure in full battle attire. His eyes have been described as "dark, penetrating and enigmatic."

Wearing the typical attire of the Morelos farmer — white pants, white shirt and sombrero — Zapatista troops enter Cuernavaca, the capital of Morelos, after defeating federal forces on August 13, 1914.

Zapata's followers, including women, swarm through a cornfield. Known as *soldaderas*, wives and girl friends accompanied their men to battle, caring for them — and even taking up the arms of the fallen.

Soldiers of the federal army
(*foreground*) exchange fire with straw-
hatted Zapatistas on a hillside.

Wrecked by Zapatistas, a locomotive lies in pieces on an embankment. Locomotives were sometimes used to pull up tracks behind retreating troops or, when loaded with dynamite, as deadly weapons to send crashing into enemy trains.

In Mexico City for the installation of a new president during a brief period of peace in December 1914, Zapata, holding his famed sombrero, sits with fellow revolutionary leader Pancho Villa in the National Palace. The two men had only recently met, and hopes ran high that they would form an alliance; but the coalition never came to pass.

VILLA EN LA SILLA PRESIDENCIAL

A gigantic painted sculpture of the
19th-century patriot Benito Juárez
forms an archway in Nezahualcóyotl, on the outskirts of Mexico City.
The sculpture, designed by Luis
Arenal, is one of many monumental
works done by post-revolutionary
artists to celebrate Mexican history.

120

AN EXPLOSION OF CREATIVITY

A French-born painter named Jean Charlot, who became a member of the Mexican avant-garde, recalled nostalgically how he, Diego Rivera and some of the other great Mexican artists of this century would in the 1920s hire a bus and take rollicking, laughter-filled junkets through the Mexican countryside, seeking out ancient works of art. "We were so noisy," Charlot remembered, "that onlookers guessed we were revolutionary generals on a spree rather than artists digging for esthetic roots."

The artists resembled the trigger-happy generals of the recent Mexican revolution in more than bibulous, deafening talk. They packed pistols for self-protection in that still-violent era and delighted in firing them off. On one such trip several rabbits were spotted beside the road, whereupon all the painters and sculptors in the bus unlimbered their weapons and began blasting away. This utterly terrified a peasant who had hitched a ride with the hospitable artists. Rivera, in one lucky shot, hit a darting hare, causing the animal to do a headfirst cartwheel. "Our frightened guest, before he could be stopped," recounted Charlot, "was doing the same out of our speeding bus."

This rough-and-tumble incident suggests the wild, headlong enthusiasm, the almost anarchic energy, that characterized the artistic upheaval that has come to be known as the Mexican Renaissance, the country's modern golden age. During the 1920s and 1930s, Mexico's writers revolutionized the nation's literature, shattering the polite conventions of earlier Mexican writing to create grittily realistic portrayals of the peasantry and of the bloody squalor of the revolutionary fighting. The painters even more vehemently repudiated the febrile, Europeanized art of the previous century to create uniquely Mexican works bursting with exuberant shapes and colors.

The impulse behind this extraordinary outburst of creativity was provided by the overthrow of the hated Porfirio Díaz regime and the subsequent social and political revolution. "It was as if," one observer said, "a huge cork had been popped." Other revolutions have inspired similar artistic expression, but few if any have brought forth such a stunning amount of work of such high quality. A number of the artists were dedicated revolutionaries and hurled themselves into the artistic fray like cultural shock troops, eager to create art that would help bring forth a new and better social system. Others were not so politically committed, but they, too, gained inspiration from the spirit of freedom and the fervent patriotism brought by the revolution.

The artists were inspired as well by a fresh realization of the wealth of Mexico's cultural past. The painters and sculptors avidly studied the great carvings and frescoes created by the ancient Mayan civilization, the powerful sculpture left by the Aztecs, and the murals

5

to be found in Mexico's many Spanish-colonial churches and shrines. The painters' overriding dream was to give birth to a new national art as noble as that of the ancient Indians.

The most famous and flamboyant of the painters was Rivera, a huge man of volcanic energy (he was more than six feet tall and weighed 300 pounds) who has been called "one of the great creators" of 20th-century art. Almost equally celebrated, imposing and prolific were his two great contemporaries, José Clemente Orozco and David Alfaro Siqueiros. Orozco's writhing images outdid even Rivera's in their expressiveness. Siqueiros' life, as well as his art, was so filled with revolutionary passion that he frequently found himself in prison. Known as "the Big Three," these great painters were the most visible vanguard of Mexico's cultural resurgence.

Born in the city of Guanajuato in Central Mexico in 1886, Rivera was a prodigy from the start. By the time he was three years old he had covered so many walls of his home with drawings that his father, a schoolteacher, provided him with a blackboard-lined room. He began studying at Mexico's national art school, the San Carlos Academy, when he was 10 and had departed before he was 16, disgusted by the school's old-fashioned curriculum, which demanded adherence to detailed realism. In 1907, when he was 20, Rivera showed several of his paintings to the governor of Veracruz, who was so impressed that he awarded the young artist a scholarship to study in Europe.

During the next decade, as his country rocked with the upheaval of revolution, Rivera was caught up in the artistic ferment of Paris, falling under the spell first of Paul Cézanne, then of Pablo Pi-

casso, Georges Braque and the other pioneers of Cubism. Rivera poured out his own Cubist paintings at a furious rate. His Paris dealer recalled that his huge Mexican client delivered "about five major pictures a month," and this did not count "sketches, pastels, watercolors and so on."

Rivera's bohemian life in Montparnasse was interrupted in 1920 when his fellow countryman Siqueiros arrived in France, fresh from fighting on Mexican battlefields. As Rivera introduced his colleague to the local art scene, Siqueiros spoke of the suffering and hope brought by the revolution and of the need for a public, monumental art that would inspire the people. The idea ignited Rivera's interest, and the two painters went off and traveled through Italy, studying the work of the great Renaissance muralists.

After a last brief sojourn in Paris, Rivera abruptly sailed for home, leaving Siqueiros behind. Back in Mexico, he found that he and Siqueiros had a powerful ally in an eccentric and visionary artist and art teacher who called himself Dr. Atl. Christened Gerardo Murillo, Atl so admired Mexico's Indian past that he had renamed himself after the Aztec word for water, and he urged his art students to study the works of the Aztecs, Mayas and their other Indian forebears. Atl had also been spellbound during his own student days in Rome by Michelangelo's awesome frescoes, and he dreamed of Sistine Chapels in his native land.

Appointed director of the government's Department of Fine Arts in 1921, Atl organized the country's first major exposition of native arts and crafts. He brought together in Chapultepec Park the entire range of Mexico's vibrant profusion of folk art, from pot-

tery and papier-mâché figures to ceramics and lacquerwork. The effect was electrifying, inspiring a new respect for the country's rich culture. He also urged Mexico's younger artists to revive the technique of fresco painting. Atl was seconded by José Vasconcelos, the new minister of public education, who helped persuade the government to let Rivera and other artists paint murals in government buildings.

Rivera, Siqueiros, Charlot and several other painters responded vigorously to the twin challenges of preaching the revolutionary gospel in paint and restoring the mural to its high place in Mexican art. Orozco, too, though less of a political activist, was an enthusiastic member of the muralist movement. "The highest form of painting, the purest, the strongest, is the mural," he announced. "It cannot be turned into an object for personal profit; it cannot be hidden for the benefit of the privileged few. It is for the people. It is for all."

Rivera painted his first mural, *The Creation,* in the amphitheater of the National Preparatory School in Mexico City in 1922, when he was 35 years old. Wearing a large cowboy hat, black miner's boots, baggy clothes and a cartridge belt, Rivera was a novel sight on the scaffold, where he was joined by a succession of beautiful models, one of whom, Guadalupe Marín, he married the same year. Watching from below, and occasionally snatching food from his lunch basket, was a gawky adolescent named Frida Kahlo who would later marry Rivera herself and become a distinguished artist in her own right.

Rivera worked with breathtaking speed, as if driven by some force outside himself. "I am not merely an artist," he explained, "but a man performing his biological function of producing

paintings, just as a tree produces flowers and fruit." He talked nonstop, entertaining friends and onlookers with outrageous and usually quite fictitious tales of derring-do, such as how he had slaughtered dozens of enemies during the Russian revolution — although he had never set foot in Russia.

Rivera did this first mural, in which giant figures personify various human virtues and arts, in encaustic — paint mixed with melted wax and fixed on the wall with heat. Thereafter he employed pure fresco technique, painting with his own hand-ground pigments on a layer of fresh and very fine plaster so that the colors soaked into the plaster and became part of the wall.

On his next project, begun in 1923, Rivera worked at times with such intensity that he exhausted teams of plasterers, whose job was to prepare the wall ahead of his speeding brush. It was a colossal undertaking: 124 frescoes depicting the Mexican people engaged in their labors and festivals, and covering the interior walls and corridors of Mexico City's huge Ministry of Public Education, a building two blocks long, one block wide and three stories high.

The task would ultimately take him more than five years to complete.

Before getting under way, Rivera embarked on his first trip to the Yucatán Peninsula and the Mayan regions of the southeast. There he vastly increased his knowledge of Mexico's heritage of pre-Columbian art and native crafts. It was the only love affair that was to last his lifetime. His dominant subject matter became Mexico's Indians and their struggle for a better life.

Sympathy for the Indians and other disadvantaged peoples made Rivera a lifelong Marxist, and for a number of years he was an official of the Mexican Communist Party. His frescoes often carried a Marxist message and were replete with red flags, hammers and sickles, and other Communist symbols. He depicted capitalists as evil men, employing harsh colors and sharp, jagged brushstrokes. Mexico's Indians, on the other hand, were painted as heroic figures with flowing brushstrokes and warm, earthy colors.

In 1926, while still completing the Ministry of Public Education murals, Rivera began what is regarded as his finest work, the frescoes at the National School of Agriculture in Chapingo, a few miles east of Mexico City. On one side of a baroque, 18th-century salon, he painted panels depicting the biological development of human life. On the other side he did murals portraying the human race's historical and social development. On one of the end walls, dominating the entire room, Rivera created a colossal reclining nude symbolizing Mother Earth.

Painted in a variety of tints applied with small brushstrokes, this nude is a noble as well as sensual figure. Critics have hailed it as one of the greatest nudes in the history of art and Rivera's masterpiece. "He would enrich his work with new subjects," observed art historian Justino Fernández, "but he would never go beyond the level he achieved at Chapingo."

The female figures in Rivera's frescoes were frequently modeled on his wives — four in all — or on his many mistresses. Despite being ugly (one wife compared him to a frog) and very fat, he was a man of such enormous vitality and charm that he attracted women in droves and lived his marital life in chaos. During a jealous rage his second wife, Lupe Marín, smashed one of Rivera's treasured pre-Columbian idols and served him the shards in his soup.

When that stormy marriage ended in 1928, Rivera embarked on an almost equally tempestuous partnership with Frida Kahlo, who had watched him paint when she was a schoolgirl. Married in 1929 when Frida was 22 and Rivera 42, they weathered many stresses and strains — and a divorce and remarriage — until Frida's death from an embolism at the age of 47.

The first months of marriage provided Frida with a hectic forecast of what life with Rivera would be like.

A tree of life rises whorl upon whorl from a Nativity scene. It is the work of famed folk potter Herón Martínez "When I design a new work," he says, "the idea will come to me during the night. I invent it in my head and translate the idea directly into clay."

These clay angels, known as *chía* figures, are placed on altars during the Easter season. Meant to encourage the growth of corn and beans, they have grooves into which lemon sage seeds are rubbed; when the angels are filled with water, the seeds sprout, evoking good harvests.

THE JOYOUS ART OF THE PEOPLE

The vividness of the Mexican imagination has gained splendid expression in the hands of folk potters. Although their output is widely collected, the artists themselves remain unassuming, devoting themselves to their production in the villages where they have always lived.

Most find their inspiration in local tales and beliefs, a potent mixture of Indian and Spanish lore. Many work in primitive conditions. One uses old tires to fuel his kiln. Another improvises some tools: "The dog gives me bristles for my paintbrush. The rooster also gives me feathers to paint with." But despite such seeming limitations, the potters are masters

of technique. At a world congress of ceramists, one of Mexico's most famous practitioners, Teodora Blanco, entered a friendly competition with a Japanese. According to her son, "The Japanese said, 'I can make a sculpture 70 centimeters tall.' 'I can make one 80,' she replied. The figure the Japanese made collapsed. My mother's was bigger and it endured."

The work of these artists may be playful, but it has its darker side, too. When asked why her skeleton figures looked happy, one woman replied, "Our life is hard. The days are long. God takes many. We do not fear death; we joke about it; we play with it. We have to do this or become bitter."

An elaborate piece by Candelario Medrano derives from a play about the defeat of the Moors by the Spaniards. Portions of the drama are still acted in his town each July 24. The figure on the left stands for "a coyote who stole corn and blamed it on Christ and the king," says Medrano.

Half animal, half witch, this figure represents a *nahual*, or guardian spirit, gone bad. According to its maker, the *nahual* here is a person by day but turns into a witch at night and steals kitchen items like the mats and grinding stones seen clinging to its side.

Two skeletons symbolize the spirits of the dead who are thought to visit their relatives on the 1st and 2nd of November each year. Such figures are used to decorate family altars on which plants and photographs of departed loved ones are also placed.

5

Within weeks of the wedding, he was appointed director of the San Carlos Academy, which he and his fellow muralists had attended as students. Characteristically, he attempted to turn the place upside down, abolishing the rigid curriculum that had smothered him as a boy. His wholesale reforms proved too much for the tradition-bound academy, and Rivera was fired less than a year after he had been hired.

In 1929 Rivera was also ousted from the Mexican Communist Party, in part because its more militant members thought he had accepted too many commissions from an increasingly anti-Communist government. Rivera was devastated but continued to paint at a superhuman pace. Between August and December he managed at last to finish the Ministry of Public Education panels, painted a series of gigantic nudes for the Ministry of Health, designed the sets and costumes for a ballet written by one of Mexico's most brilliant young composers, Carlos Chávez, and began his epic murals at the National Palace depicting the history of the Mexican people from ancient times to the present. "Work is his entertainment," concluded Frida, who regularly visited her husband on the scaffold in order to see him at all.

By this time Rivera's fame had spread to the United States. In 1931, New York's Museum of Modern Art honored him with a retrospective exhibition, which drew the largest attendance (56,575) of any show the museum had held up to that time. Rivera, who had already painted an *Allegory of California* at, improbably, the San Francisco Stock Exchange, now received a flurry of commissions from other capitalist bastions. His U.S. patrons chose—at least initially—to overlook

his openly Marxist message and unflattering depictions of capitalism. They did so on the seemingly sound public relations ground that anyone willing to pay for Rivera's acknowledged artistry would appear to be more interested in the public good than private gain—a desirable image in the early years of the Depression. Rivera viewed his U.S. commissions as a glittering opportunity to create public art glorifying the industrial proletariat.

As a patron-artist relationship, it was doomed from the start—and the collision was not long in coming. Rivera's third big U.S. commission caused an uproar. It was a series of frescoes at the Detroit Institute of Arts portraying the wonders of modern science and industry. Most offensive to the local clergy and a host of self-appointed critics was a panel showing the benefits of vaccination. The child being vaccinated resembled Renaissance paintings of the infant Jesus, golden halo and all, and the entire panel was modeled on a Nativity scene. Rivera was roundly denounced by press and pulpit for what was seen as a blasphemous portrayal of the Holy Family in a modern medical setting.

Despite this hostility, Rivera optimistically headed for New York, where he had been commissioned by John D. Rockefeller's then-young grandson Nelson—later a governor of New York and U.S. vice president—to paint a mural inside the main entrance of the new RCA Building in Rockefeller Center. Rivera envisioned a large fresco that would depict on the left a group of greedy businessmen enjoying a spree while the common people suffer the evils of war and unemployment. On the right was to be a Marxist utopia featuring a large portrait of Lenin.

When the mural was two-thirds fin-

ished, a New York newspaper had seen enough to publish an angry story headlined, "Rivera Paints Scenes of Communist Activity and John D. Foots Bill." Suddenly the atmosphere at Rockefeller Center grew hostile. The number of guards was increased, some of whom began to harass Rivera's plasterers and other helpers. Finally Nelson Rockefeller fired Rivera, sending him a check for the remaining $14,000 due on their $21,000 contract. A screen of tarpaper was put up to hide the offending mural, and it was later chiseled off the wall. (The present murals were done by the Spanish artist José María Sert and the British painter Frank Brangwyn.)

Furious at being fired, Rivera got some satisfaction after he had returned

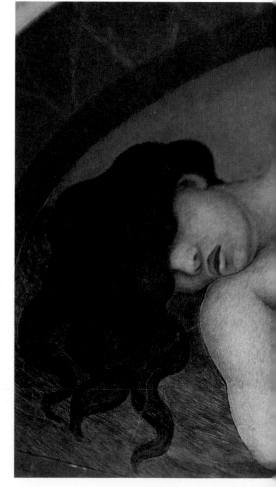

A wall-size Mother Earth shelters a seedling in this detail from Diego Rivera's masterpiece, the frescoes for the Agricultural School at Chapingo. He dedicated the work "to all those who fell and the thousands who will yet fall in the fight for the land."

home by reproducing the Rockefeller Center mural in Mexico City's Palace of Fine Arts. He used some of the money earned in the U.S. to build a pair of connected houses in the Mexico City suburb of San Angel—one for Frida, one for himself and his studio. These homes and one in nearby Coyoacán became places of pilgrimage for artists and art lovers from around the world.

Despite the distractions brought by fame and a period of poor health that slowed him down, Rivera ultimately resumed work with his accustomed energy, sometimes spending 15 hours straight on a scaffold. And he retained his ability to set off public uproars to the end of his life. The greatest pandemonium of his career occurred in 1948 when his mural with the placid title *Dream of a Sunday Afternoon in the Alameda* was unveiled at Mexico City's Del Prado Hotel. It showed the heroes and villains of Mexican history on a Sunday stroll, which nobody objected to. But it also contained the words *"Dios no existe"*—"God does not exist." This inflamed Catholic Mexico, and outraged mobs besieged the hotel, determined to destroy the painting. The uproar continued until the government finally boarded it over.

The mural remained hidden until 1956, when Rivera at last agreed to remove the offending phrase. He did so one April evening as the press and a throng of onlookers watched from below. Finally climbing laboriously down from the scaffold, Rivera, in true form, startled everyone with the announcement: "I am a Catholic." (He had in fact been brought up in the church by his pious mother, but most of his friends doubted that he had really returned to the fold.)

Rivera died of cancer the following year at the age of 70. Not even his funeral was immune from fracas; a squabble broke out among his relatives about the Communist Party's participation in the ceremonies.

Rivera's life, for all its storms, was almost tranquil when compared with that of his colleague Siqueiros, the youngest of the three great mural painters. Volatile and defiantly militant, Siqueiros announced his presence on Mexico's artis-

A detail from Diego Rivera's mural *Dream of a Sunday Afternoon* shows the artist as a boy being led by a surrealist figure of death. Behind him is his wife Frida. Rivera mixed characters out of history with those out of his own life in this major work.

tic scene by helping, at the age of 14, to stage a 1911 student strike against the fusty curriculum at the San Carlos Academy. He later recalled with mock innocence that all he had done "was join the bigger boys to see how it was done and throw stones at people." Still, Siqueiros was one of the few participants to wind up behind bars.

It was far from the last time. An indefatigable agitator, Siqueiros harbored unbounded contempt for the law, and arrests for political dissidence became almost routine. His penchant for fighting found other outlets. During the revolution he joined one of the contending armies and became an officer while still a teenager. In 1936 he went to Spain to fight in that country's civil war, ending up a divisional commander in the Republican Army.

Back in Mexico in 1940, Siqueiros leaped from the art pages into world headlines. He was one of a group of would-be assassins who, on behalf of the Soviet Union's vengeful leader, Josef Stalin, attempted unsuccessfully to machine-gun Stalin's old rival for power, the exiled Red Army leader Leon Trotsky. Creeping up on Trotsky's refuge, a villa in a Mexico City suburb, the gunmen riddled the house but missed their intended victim; Trotsky and his wife had dived under a bed for protection. Siqueiros was jailed only briefly — because, some claim, high-ranking friends intervened. In any case, he never denied his involvement in the shooting spree. (The unfortunate Trotsky was later murdered by a single killer wielding a simpler weapon, a mountaineer's ice ax.)

Siqueiros was as impatient with artistic restrictions as he was with the law. He was the first of the Mexican muralists to apply color with a spray gun and to experiment with new synthetic materials such as acrylics. He also sought new subject matter. "I say we have had enough of pretty pictures of grinning peons in traditional dress and carrying baskets on their backs," he once declared, taking a jab at Rivera. "I say to hell with oxcarts — let's see more tractors and bulldozers."

Caught up like Rivera in Dr. Atl's enthusiasm for mural painting, Siqueiros began his major work as Rivera had by decorating walls in the National Preparatory School. Siqueiros' first panels were apolitical, treating such themes as the four elements of fire, air, earth and water. But then a 1922 Mexican workers' strike, violently suppressed by the government, inspired a brooding prolabor fresco called *Burial of a Worker*. This mural was so clearly antigovernment that Siqueiros was ejected from the Preparatory School in 1924 while still engaged in painting it. From then until 1930 the artist hardly touched a brush; instead, he devoted all his formidable energies to labor organization.

He returned to painting during a seven-month jail term in 1930 and the period of police surveillance that followed, producing with Rivera-like gus-

In a painting by Frida Kahlo, third wife of Diego Rivera, the artist shyly gives her hand to her hulking husband. Frida, a self-taught primitive, documented the couple's stormy marriage beginning with this, a portrait of their wedding day.

to about 100 easel paintings. Then, offered a choice of more time in jail or self-exile, Siqueiros moved temporarily to Los Angeles, where he earned a living teaching at an art school and executing some murals. Returning to Mexico in 1934, he continued mural painting, his first love, and in 1939 produced on the walls of Mexico City's Electrical Workers Union one of his masterpieces, a powerful series of panels attacking fascism.

In the late 1940s and the 1950s Siqueiros enjoyed a relatively peaceful interlude during which he completed major murals — on militantly proletarian subjects — in Mexico City's Treasury Building, National University and Social Security Hospital No. 1. "A muralist must have a theme," he declared, echoing Dr. Atl and Rivera. "His mural is his pulpit."

Age in no fashion mellowed Siqueiros. At 64, while at work on a 175-foot panel in Mexico City's Chapultepec Castle, he was arrested and charged once again with inciting riots. At his trial, he mesmerized the observers with a three-hour speech on his youthful years in politics, the panorama of Mexican painting and the betrayal of the 1910-1920 Revolution by every subsequent regime. He also threw in several personal insults aimed at the presiding judge. Sentenced to eight years, Siqueiros served almost four, painting prodigiously except when organizing an inmate baseball team — on which he played first base.

Siqueiros' final project, undertaken when he was 70, was a colossal mural in the auditorium of Mexico City's Hotel de Mexico that covered a staggering area of 50,000 square feet. It bore the characteristically grandiose title *The March of Humanity on Earth toward the*

Cosmos. Soon after he had completed this work, Siqueiros died of cancer at the age of 77.

José Clemente Orozco, the oldest of the Big Three, was in some ways the opposite of his famous colleagues. While Rivera and Siqueiros thrived on conflict and public display, Orozco avoided controversy and treasured his own privacy. He was also less militant politically and, although he often did employ Mexican subject matter, he attempted to use it to express more universal meanings.

When he began painting, in fact, Orozco openly disdained painters who were, as he said, "tickled silly at the sight of our Mexican pots and pans."

Born in 1883, he grew up in Mexico City. Orozco remained a devoted urban dweller all his life, and he initially devoted his art to satirical portrayals of the modern metropolis.

Orozco's family opposed his artistic ambitions at first, sending him to the National School of Agriculture in San Jacinto. But Orozco detested the bucolic life and rebelled against his family's wishes. An accidental explosion in a chemistry laboratory, which cost him his left hand and the partial sight of one eye, only confirmed his devotion to the artistic life. Artists were "poor devils," he said, and his maimed condition now qualified him as "one of them."

In 1906, at the age of 23, Orozco be-

gan an intensive period of study at the San Carlos Academy. His first works were scenes of the seedier side of city life. "Instead of red and yellow twilights," he later recalled, "I painted pestilent shadows of closed rooms" and "drunken ladies and gentlemen."

Orozco's early studies of the underside of urban life jolted the public. "Orozco's art is disquieting, spectral, tortured," wrote poet and painter Raziel Cabildo. "These are nightmarish watercolors where human monsters shake in a convulsive dance their rotted flesh, amidst an asphyxiating fog compounded of alcohol fumes, tobacco and stale pomade." Orozco's experiences in the revolution, during which he wit-

Contorted figures from a mural in relief entitled *The March of Humanity* dwarf David Alfaro Siqueiros, the artist. This monumental work covers the walls and ceiling of a many-sided auditorium named for him in Mexico City.

nessed some scenes of frightful slaughter, electrified his art. His bitter caricatures, filled with a sense of the macabre, became even more lethal than before.

Orozco's biting works were greeted with public indignation, and he sold few of them at his first one-man show in 1916. Disillusioned, he packed a portfolio of watercolors and chanced a trip to the United States, where he hoped for a better reception. To his horror, many of his vivid paintings of Mexico City night life were ripped to shreds before his eyes by U.S. customs officials at the border who took one look and, with puritanical zeal, decreed Orozco's art "immoral." He finally made his way to New York. There, unable to sell the few works the customs inspectors had spared and living in extreme poverty, he survived by working in a doll factory, painting complexions with an airbrush, and eyes and lashes by hand.

Orozco managed to save enough of his pay to get back to Mexico City. He became primarily a newspaper cartoonist, convinced that the public was incapable of appreciating his painting. The significance of his serious work was being recognized, however, by a growing number of influential people — most notably a Mexican poet and newspaper columnist, José Juan Tablada, who called Orozco "the greatest of our Mexican painters." Almost singlehandedly, Tablada forced the government to offer Orozco a commission for mural painting.

Orozco was 40 years old when he began his first frescoes on several walls of that much-decorated edifice, the National Preparatory School. "My one theme is humanity; my one tendency is emotion to a maximum," he told an interviewer as he got under way on panels portraying the revolutionary struggle, the ancient races of Mexico and the Spanish Conquest. His scenes of violence were later compared to the great Spanish artist Francisco Goya's grisly series of etchings called *The Disasters of War*. One critic stated flatly that Orozco's frescoes were "the greatest mural painting since the early Italians."

As in the past, the public response was less enthusiastic. An early version of one mural showed a nude woman that Orozco said represented motherhood but a number of observers took to be a blasphemous Madonna. The uproar this caused was multiplied when another part of Orozco's work portrayed the Spanish conquistadors as benefactors of the Mexican Indians. Orozco, with characteristic contrariness, believed that the Conquest had been beneficial, but this was a very unpopular interpretation of Mexican history. Angry student mobs attacked the frescoes, bombarding them with stones, decayed vegetables and rotten eggs. Only after petitions were signed by thousands of Mexican and foreign art lovers did Orozco consent to return to the Preparatory School to repair the damage and finish the murals, which were completed in 1927.

Late that same year the artist journeyed once again to New York, there to begin an intense period of easel painting. In April 1929, a widely publicized exhibition of his paintings and drawings was given at New York's Art Students League to highly approving reviews. This success led to several private commissions.

Not until the mid-1930s did Orozco return to Mexico City, where he painted *Catharsis* at the Palace of Fine Arts; it is a mural that employs violent forms to express what the artist perceived as the horror and corruption of the modern world. Orozco then launched a series of major projects 400 miles away in Guadalajara. He first decorated the enormous cupola of the University of Guadalajara. Working 125 feet above the floor, he completed a large fresco that celebrates the various achievements of mankind. He then did the imposing stairway of the Palace of Government; the murals trace Mexico's struggle for political freedom from the 1810 revolt against Spanish rule through the revolution and its aftermath.

In the stairway painting — as in much of Orozco's work — swirling, lurid flames surround many of the human figures. The artist's last fresco in Guadalajara, considered his masterpiece, covers the vast walls and dome of the chapel of Hospicio Cabañas, an 18th-century home for orphaned children. The overall theme of this huge work is human evolution.

With money earned from another visit to the U.S., Orozco built a new studio in Mexico City and set about designing frescoes for the walls of the city's National Supreme Court Building and the former chapel of a Jesuit hospital. The theme of these would be justice for Mexico's workers. Painting them was not easy. Visitors watching Orozco at work in the chapel were appalled to see the 60-year-old one-handed artist struggling to make the 50-foot climb to the scaffold. Orozco seemed totally unperturbed, however, and as one observer noted, simply "lifted a bucket of brushes and colors from the end of his stump and began to draw."

Orozco remained active until the end of his life. He was just beginning a new mural called *Primavera* on the garden wall of a Mexico City housing project in September 1949 when he grew unaccountably weary and left early for home. He died that evening of heart failure at the age of 65.

His funeral was a national event, attended by thousands of his fellow citizens. An American witnessing the event was impressed by the crowds of ordinary people who came to pay homage. "I dare say," he later wrote, "that more than one foreigner thought what a wonderful thing it was for an artist to be a citizen of a country where, if he was a great artist, he could be a great man."

In the end Orozco and his fellow muralists, for all the public clamor that their works and lives occasioned, did succeed in realizing their dream of creating a new national art of epic power and proportions. "They painted in another way," wrote Mexican art historian Rafael Carrillo, "and consequently taught us how to observe in a different way; they changed how our eyes moved, freeing us of old conventions, confirming the dignity of our fate by exalting the ordinary man."

Not all of the painters of Mexico's golden age were muralists. The most notable exception was Rufino Tamayo, who favored easel painting most of his life. He also rejected his great contemporaries' emphasis on politics. He was, Tamayo said, "against everything that attempts to put art at the service of any goal other than man himself, in his totality," and he went so far as to add that the muralists were "engaged in journalism, not painting; they gave classes in sociology, history." But Tamayo's work was nevertheless in its own way as bold and unsettling as theirs.

Though Tamayo criticized the muralists' preoccupation with Indian subject matter, he was himself a Zapotec and grew up in humble circumstances. Born in Oaxaca in 1899, he was orphaned as an adolescent, going to live

5

with an aunt who ran a fruit business in Mexico City. He became fascinated with the city's open-air markets, especially the vibrant colors and tropical abundance of the stalls full of mangoes, papayas, pineapples and watermelons. They would later appear in his exuberant still-life paintings.

Tamayo's prudent aunt enrolled her nephew in a commercial school to study business. Tamayo regularly skipped school, however, and instead attended classes at the San Carlos Academy, paying his tuition and supporting himself by working at the National Archeology Museum. After three years at the academy, he studied some more on his own, intently analyzing the painterly tech-

niques of the French Impressionists, Post-Impressionists and Cubists. Only they, he said, had "the vitality to nourish and stimulate." Soon he had become the champion of a small antimuralist minority and had staged his first one-man show in a rented shop on Avenida Madero. Three years later, in 1929, he held his second Mexico City show. It included *Chair with Fruit,* Tamayo's first indisputable masterpiece, an extraordinarily effective grouping of the simple objects named in the title.

The unobtrusive Tamayo did not make much of a splash — or earn much money — in the noisy, fizzing art world of Mexico City. So he and his new wife, pianist Olga Flores Rivas, left for New

York in 1936. There the artist earned a livelihood teaching art at a Manhattan private day school. He was to remain in the U.S. until 1949.

He and Olga then moved to Paris, center of the Cubist and Impressionist movements that had been the artist's inspiration. Paris lionized Tamayo, but the painter had mixed feelings about that beautiful but often gray and rainy city. "I didn't feel happy living there even though I was a success from the start," he said. "I, who am supposed to be a colorist, was almost reduced to painting everything in black. It's because I was in the wrong place. Then a very curious thing happened. When I went back to Mexico — immediately the

132

first picture I began to paint was full of color once more."

Back in Mexico City, the Tamayos designed for themselves a suburban house with a garden abounding in the colors the painter had made his trademark. Mixing his own pigments and working in a cobbler's apron, Tamayo painted as if he were a craftsman instead of an artist. "I don't believe you can work only if you are inspired," he once said. "I think the inspiration is in the work itself. So I work like any laborer, seven or eight hours a day."

The revolution in painting wrought by Rivera and his contemporaries was paralleled by an upheaval in Mexican literature. The first writer to explode the old literary conventions was, improbably enough, an obscure middle-aged physician named Mariano Azuela. Born in Jalisco in 1873, Azuela received his medical degree in Guadalajara in 1899. In 1910 he became an ardent supporter of the revolution, ending up as a field doctor with the forces of Pancho Villa. After Villa suffered crushing defeats in the spring of 1915, Azuela fled across the border into Texas.

It was there, in the cramped, steamy printing shop of an El Paso newspaper, that Azuela wrote his historic novel *The Underdogs*. The newspaper, a Spanish-language daily, published the work in installments, offering the author only a few dollars and some copies of his work in return.

In this version the novel, as one critic put it, "escaped the attention of practically everyone." When it was finally published in Mexico City a decade later, however, its impact was overwhelming. Recognized as the definitive novel of the revolution, it also launched an entire literary movement.

The novel's impact came from its un-

Rufino Tamayo, who unlike many of his contemporaries was not interested in art as a vehicle of social protest, painted this *Portrait of Olga,* his wife, in the warm tones he loved.

sparing realism. As a field physician, Azuela had been afforded a close-up view of the revolution's destructive and dehumanizing effects. He had also noted that it was the idealists more often than not who got killed, leaving the opportunists in control. This disillusion reverberates through *The Underdogs,* which tells the story of a simple peasant, Demetrio Macías, who becomes caught up in the revolution's seemingly endless bloodshed without knowing what he is fighting for. To emphasize the pointlessness, Azuela has his hero die on the same spot of ground that was the scene of his faction's first victory. "Demetrio Macías," the novel's last sentence reads, "eyes fixed forever, keeps aiming his rifle."

The Underdogs broke with literary conventions not only in content, but also in style. Azuela employed none of the plots and subplots or the elevated literary language that had made Mexican novels tedious copies of European models. Instead, Azuela told the story

in unadorned episodes and a terse, almost staccato prose. Most significantly, when Demetrio Macías spoke, it was in his own language, the simple, everyday speech of the common folk.

Azuela's stark narrative provoked an avalanche of novels about the revolution told in the same unromantic fashion. One of the best, *The Eagle and the Serpent,* was the work of Martín Luis Guzmán, a journalist born in Chihuahua in 1887. Like Azuela, Guzmán was initially in favor of the revolution, abandoning a comfortable existence as a university student to join Pancho Villa. Captivated for a time by Villa's charismatic personality, Guzmán eventually grew weary of Villa's penchant for violence and pillage, and his disillusionment is mirrored in his novel, which is a fictionalized account of his own experiences of the revolutionary fighting.

A brilliant second generation of modern Mexican writers has, like Azuela and Guzmán, remained committed to the ideals of the revolution while questioning its methods and its results. One of the most controversial new writers has been Carlos Fuentes, whose novels were once described by an English critic as "exotic, erotic and experimental."

Born in 1928, Fuentes began writing in the early 1950s and published his first novel, *Where the Air Is Clear,* in 1958. The title, taken from a phrase used by a 19th-century scientist to describe the Mexico City of his day, is bitterly ironical. The book is an acid portrait of greed and corruption at all levels of Mexico City's society in the middle part of the 20th century. It condemns the revolution for ultimately failing the Mexican people — with the exception of the fast-living *nouveaux riches* who were, Fuentes believed, the only ones to profit from it.

Fuentes explored the same theme in his third novel, *The Death of Artemio Cruz,* which tells the story of a revolutionary patriot, Cruz, who becomes one of the nation's exploiters. A technical tour de force, the book focuses on the final 12 hours of Cruz's life. Lying on his deathbed, he reviews the key events that led him from humble beginnings in a thatched hut on a coffee plantation to his eventual apotheosis as a feared tycoon and politician, willing to trample anyone in his path.

This portrait of a man who sold out his ideals, betraying the revolution, his homeland and eventually himself, owes a substantial philosophical debt to an older writer, Octavio Paz, perhaps Mexico's most respected contemporary thinker. Born on the outskirts of Mexico City in 1914, Paz was already a well-known figure in the capital's intellectual circles by the age of 18. Much of his best poetry, then and since, reflects Paz's feelings about himself and about Mexico. He expresses these in difficult, allusive verse that owes debts to the French symbolists of the late 19th century, especially Stéphane Mallarmé, and to the surrealists of this century.

The subtlety of his early poetry and of his essays earned Paz international recognition, and he was awarded a Guggenheim Fellowship in 1943 to live and study in the United States for two years. Looking back at Mexico from New York with the perspective of distance, Paz began to see his native land as a country haunted by its violent history and constantly betrayed by its leaders — a nation whose people live in a state of perpetual distrust and isolation. These perceptions he elaborated in a book-length series of linked essays that is considered to be his prose master-

piece, *Labyrinth of Solitude,* published in 1950. In it he also suggested that the Mexicans' search for an identity and their stoicism in the face of life's cruelties is perhaps the paradigm of all human existence.

Paz's fame as poet and essayist also earned him high rank in Mexico's diplomatic service, a not unusual circumstance in a country that has accorded its intellectuals an unusual degree of respect and has often rewarded them with high government posts. (Fuentes, too, was a diplomat and for a time Mexico's ambassador to France.) Diplomatic service in such varied places as France and India served to widen and enrich Paz's already formidable imagination and store of poetic images. He emerged from his ambassadorial role in 1968 not only as an even more widely respected poet, but as a perceptive critic of art and literature as well.

A far more private and retiring figure has been a writer who, in the eyes of history, may be judged Mexico's greatest modern author. This is Juan Rulfo, born in 1918 in the hot and largely desolate southern part of the state of Jalisco. Orphaned at 12, Rulfo spent the rest of his youth in an orphanage that was more like a reformatory.

Released from this "boarding school," as Rulfo mordantly termed it, the homeless, rootless young man did odd jobs in Mexico City until he got a minor post in 1935 with Mexico's immigration service. Moving from one job to another, Rulfo ended up in 1962 in the Indian Institute, an organization that has tried to protect and aid Mexico's more primitive Indian peoples.

Somehow Rulfo found time during intervals in his various jobs to write a series of short stories, collected under the title *The Burning Plain* in 1953,

and a 125-page novel named after its villain, *Pedro Páramo,* published in 1955. Both of these thin volumes became instant classics and vaulted their author to the front rank of Latin American writers. By one recent count, a million copies of *Pedro Páramo* had been printed and sold.

Both the stories and the novel present a bleak, not to say nightmarish, picture of life in the blighted rural Mexico that Rulfo knew as a boy and revisited countless times afterward. It is a land living under a curse — much like the southern United States as pictured by William Faulkner — dating back to the cruelty and greed shown by some of the original Spanish conquerors.

One of the stories tells how a group of poor peasants, promised land during the post-revolution breakup of the great haciendas, must trek for 11 hours across an empty wasteland to locate the desolate plots they have been assigned by the authorities — who have reserved for themselves the fertile areas bordering a river. Arriving at last, the weary men find the ground so hard that no plow can break it. "Nothing will rise" from this stony soil, one of them says, "not even vultures." In another tale, an exhausted fugitive learns that the soldiers searching for him have taken out their frustration over not finding him by murdering his uncles.

Rulfo's brief, surreal novel concerns a young man's search for his father, the Pedro Páramo of the title, who had long since deserted the boy and his mother. He locates his renegade father in a distant town that, he discovers, is inhabited solely by dead people. The citizens have died, it turns out, because his dying father — the epitome of a murderous and rapacious village *caudillo* — has in a final burst of malice cut

Brightly stuccoed walls combine to become a work of art in this sharply angled private stable with pool. The complex is the work of Luis Barragán, one of Mexico's leading contemporary architects.

off all the village's food supplies. The son, as if infected by the ghosts of the starved villagers, dies as well.

These tales, grim as they are, burst into astonishing life through the dazzlingly original and imaginative way Rulfo tells them. In the novel especially, the dead walk among the living; dream, hallucination and reality mix and blend; time bends and backs up and flows again. Yet Rulfo, for all his phantasmagorical techniques, employs — like his literary forebear Azuela — only the simplest language, the everyday speech of the people of rural Mexico. "I don't want to speak as you write," Rulfo once said, "but to write as you speak." And his spare prose often has the devastating ring of utter finality — "quick glimpses," as one critic put it, "into the soul of ruin."

There seems sparse hope in Rulfo's Mexico, but there is always promise for the future in an imagination of such vigor, in an artistic mastery so impressive. And Rulfo's work, according to some critics, marks by its uncompromising Mexican-ness the final expulsion of European influence on Mexican art and literature. Rulfo, in this view, has finished the task undertaken by the artists and writers of the revolutionary era, to create a truly native culture. □

In a banner-hung plaza, future voters from the town of Aguascalientes attend a huge government-sponsored rally before the election of Miguel de la Madrid Hurtado as Mexico's president in 1982. Since Mexico has only one effective political party, its candidate is assured of victory.

THE RIDDLE OF MEXICAN POLITICS

On the morning of September 1, 1982, President José López Portillo summoned top-rank officials to an unprecedented meeting just hours before he was to deliver his annual state-of-the-nation address, and only three months before he was to relinquish office to a successor already elected. Clearly a grave decision was to be announced. How this decision was made and then implemented tells much about Mexico, whose political and economic system may be unique in the world.

The 20 cabinet ministers and 30 agency heads who gathered that day expected the president to take some step to remedy the nation's sorely depressed economy. Heavy debt and staggering inflation were only two of the ills; compounding the malaise were dropping oil revenues and an alarming shift of capital from Mexico to foreign financial havens (at least $14 billion had already left the country, according to López Portillo). Despite the immensity of these problems, few in the room were prepared for López Portillo's announcement: The government was taking over the country's 54 private banks.

The president — though obviously aware of the impact his decision would have — had not bothered to solicit advice beforehand; only one cabinet minister had been consulted, and only six had been informed of the decision prior to its announcement. Even López Portillo's successor, Miguel de la Madrid Hurtado, did not hear of the deci-

sion until the night before it was announced. And now, without having the actual decree first read aloud, López Portillo was asking for assenting signatures. "Those who want to sign can," he said. "Those who don't will be left by the wayside of history."

One official, Adrian Lajous, head of the Banco de Comercio Exterior, spoke up. *"Señor Presidente,"* he said, "I want to know if the fact that you want us to support this measure implies that we may express our opinions about it?" López Portillo's answer was abrupt: "No, either take it or leave it." Lajous' protest was the only one made that day, even though many ministers privately disagreed with the presidential move.

Thus, in one stroke, López Portillo had expanded the government's control over the economy. Not only could it now regulate interest rates and business loans more closely, it could also halt the flight of capital to foreign countries. Furthermore, since the banks held a controlling interest in many private corporations, the ownership of these now effectively passed into government hands.

López Portillo's dramatic move also had important political ramifications. In focusing attention, as the president put it, on "a group of Mexicans, supported by the private banks," who had "looted" the country, he had found a scapegoat for his earlier failure to remedy the country's ills. At the same time, he hoped to guarantee himself a place

6

in history through the boldness of his action, as President Lázaro Cárdenas had done 44 years before when he nationalized the oil industry.

As might be expected, the response to López Portillo's move was mixed. The president of the Association of Bankers of Mexico charged that it would "aggravate the current crisis"; leftist leaders praised it, maintaining that nationalization of the banks would strengthen the economy. But other strong measures would have to be taken as well, including another devaluation of the peso, for recovery to begin.

People were quick to perceive how such radical change would affect them personally. Well-heeled members of the middle class realized that currency restrictions and devaluation would cut the value of their savings. Everybody was worried that inflation would shrink their real incomes. And the labor unions feared, with good reason, that there would be reductions in jobs and in worker benefits.

Nevertheless, most politicians, the bureaucracy and the labor unions soon came around and supported the president. The Senate and Chamber of Deputies amended the constitution to legalize the nationalization of the banks, and the Supreme Court obligingly delayed lawsuits challenging López Portillo's action until the constitutional amendment had been passed. When the president called upon his party, the Partido Revolucionario Institucional (PRI), for a public demonstration of support, 500,000 people turned out for a rally in Mexico City. Attendance was not exactly voluntary — at least for anyone who expected to keep his job. PRI members who represented the labor unions, civil service and farm workers distributed little cards that had to

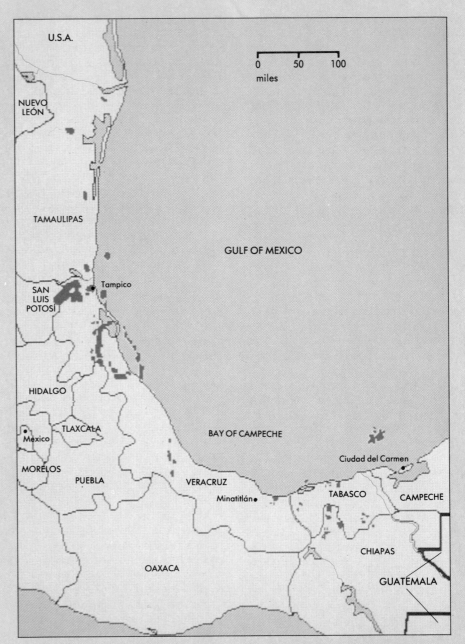

WHERE MEXICO'S OIL LIES

"We found a small, conical hill — where bubbled a spring of oil," wrote American oilman Edward L. Doheny, of a wondrous discovery that led to Mexico's first oil field in 1901. Centuries before, the Aztecs had burned oil in ceremonies and the Spaniards had used it to caulk their ships. But no one, not even Doheny, had any inkling of the true magnitude of Mexico's oil reserves. Subsequent exploration revealed supplies so vast as to raise Mexico to the status of a major oil producer. The map shows the fields being exploited there today.

be filled out and turned in afterward. Plainly, the Mexican president is extraordinarily powerful. He, more than anyone else in the country, has the final word. Although the constitution provides for an elected legislature and an independent judiciary, the president rules like an Aztec emperor. He is accorded a respect that borders on worship, and his actions are rarely challenged. In Mexico the president serves a six-year term, the *sexenio;* he cannot be reelected, but he remains supreme right up to the end.

The modern Mexican president presides over a country beset by a host of problems that seem to defy solution — unemployment, overpopulation, corruption at every level of society. His job is made no easier by the fact that the country is a bundle of contradictions. Mexico is poor, with a per capita income less than one fifth that of France; yet its industrial base is large, growing and sophisticated, and its eastern shores conceal a buried treasure of oil — more extensive reserves than any other country save Saudi Arabia. Even before nationalization of the banks, much of Mexico's business and industry was government-owned, including not only the oil industry, but also such small-fry operations as paper-bag and dish manufacturers. The rest was more or less closely regulated. Yet instead of being a handicap, government regulation has often proved a boon to rich businessmen, thanks partly to low corporate taxes levied by the government on their operations.

The paradoxes apply to politics as well. Mexicans regard their form of government as a democracy, but the term should be amended by the word "guided." In Mexico's guided democracy, there is only one political party of

real consequence: the PRI, to which all presidents since 1929 have belonged. It was founded on the sound principle that if the contending factions in the 1910 revolution were to achieve the ideals for which they had fought, they would have to bury their differences and work together. By providing the government with an ideological base of support and an apparatus through which political rewards could be distributed, the PRI has managed in the years since its foundation to stabilize a nation once racked by political chaos.

The closest rival to the PRI is the conservative Partido Acción Nacional (PAN), which in the 1985 elections won enough votes to be allotted 32 of the 100 seats reserved for minority parties in the 400-member Chamber of Deputies. Among the other political groups are the Unified Socialist Party of Mexico, a conglomeration of Marxist organizations, and the right-wing Democratic Mexican Party. In addition, there are the left-leaning Popular Socialist Party, the Socialist Workers Party and the Revolutionary Workers Party.

In another of those typically Mexican paradoxes, the PRI — the party of the revolution — is dominated by the middle class, and so is the government.

As the embodiment of the party as well as the leader of the country, the president is not just a figure to be respected; he is also to be feared. During the three months of office remaining to López Portillo after nationalization of the banks, rumors circulated that he was mobilizing the military for a coup that would keep him in office and shunt aside his elected successor. But on December 1, 1982, Inauguration Day, López Portillo marched into the monumental Chamber of Deputies and, following tradition, handed over the

green, white and red presidential sash to Miguel de la Madrid Hurtado. De la Madrid walked out of the auditorium firmly in command of the country, leaving López Portillo, his shoulders visibly sagging, to push his way through the crowd. His power had vanished with the office.

"Mexicans avoid personal dictatorships," wrote the American political scientist Frank Brandenburg, "by retiring their dictators every six years." Nothing could be more Mexican than the way a new president comes to office. Although he is elected by popular vote, the plebiscite merely ratifies a *fait accompli.* The candidate is preselected by the outgoing president, the key actor, in a secretive process called *tapadismo.* The president chooses his successor from a list of candidates acceptable to the handful of people who wield the most political power: key members of the PRI, labor leaders and the president's own circle of advisers. As time goes on, everyone knows — or thinks he does — the names on the list; but no one knows who will actually be nominated until the president informs the PRI of his choice, *El Tapado,* the Hidden One.

When López Portillo was named, he was so little known to the public that reporters attending his first press conference had to ask his wife's profession (pianist) and his children's names (José Ramón, Carmen and Paulina). But to the outgoing president, Luis Echeverría Alvarez, he was an old and favored colleague. López Portillo and Echeverría had attended the National Autonomous University of Mexico (UNAM) together, and as young men they traveled by ship to Chile, where they studied political science at the University of Santiago.

Ostensibly, López Portillo was select-

The National Palace, which has a
quiet, arcaded courtyard at its core,
functions as the president's office.

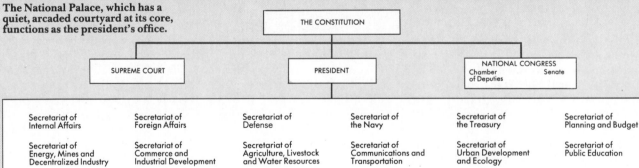

THE CONSTITUTION		
SUPREME COURT	PRESIDENT	NATIONAL CONGRESS Chamber of Deputies · Senate

Secretariat of Internal Affairs	Secretariat of Foreign Affairs	Secretariat of Defense	Secretariat of the Navy	Secretariat of the Treasury	Secretariat of Planning and Budget
Secretariat of Energy, Mines and Decentralized Industry	Secretariat of Commerce and Industrial Development	Secretariat of Agriculture, Livestock and Water Resources	Secretariat of Communications and Transportation	Secretariat of Urban Development and Ecology	Secretariat of Public Education
Secretariat of Health and Public Assistance	Secretariat of Labor and Social Security	Secretariat of the Agrarian Reform	Secretariat of Tourism	Department of the Federal District	Attorney-General

THE GOVERNMENT IN PROFILE

The Mexican government is divided
by the constitution into executive, legis-
lative and judicial branches. The
president, who holds most of the power,
is elected to a nonrenewable six-year
term. The Congress, or lawmaking body,
is composed of two houses: the Senate, with 64 members (two from each
state and two from the Federal District), and the Chamber of Deputies,
with 400 members. The senators
serve six years, the deputies three.
While 300 of the deputies are elected,
like the senators, by popular vote, 100
come to the office through propor-
tional representation (any party garner-
ing at least 1.5 percent of the popular
vote gets a like share of the 100 seats).
The Supreme Court has 21 members,
who are appointed by the president,
with Senate approval.

ed because he had done exemplary work as finance minister in Echeverría's cabinet. He won out, Echeverría claimed, "because he was the one with the fewest political attachments, the one who had not reached any secret or discreet agreements, the one who dedicated himself to the service of the country without engaging in cheap politics." Most observers, however, thought Echeverría chose his friend in the expectation of retaining some influence. If so, those hopes proved futile; within months of taking office, the new president banished his mentor to political exile by naming him ambassador to UNESCO in Paris, and a year later he made him ambassador to Australia.

Since the choosing of successors is essentially a private matter, no one knows precisely the considerations that go into the selection of *El Tapado*. At times, the choice seems made on whim. The arbitrariness of the process was documented by the historian Daniel Cosío Villegas. In 1958, the then-president, Adolfo Ruiz Cortines, gave his reaction to each name on a list of candidates as it was read aloud to him by Agustín Olachea Aviles, head of the PRI.

"Angel Carvajal . . ." began Olachea.

The president responded thoughtfully: "We love this countryman of ours a great deal, we know him well. We will not analyze why we know him well!"

"Flores Muñoz . . ."

"A very hard choice! A very good friend, a very good worker."

"Doctor Morones Prieto . . ."

"Ah! Honest like Juárez, austere like Juárez, patriotic like Juárez," commented the president, referring to the great 19th-century hero.

After Olachea finished reading the list, the president asked him if anyone had spoken of Adolfo López Mateos,

the Secretary of Labor, and the party head replied, "That one is very young, Mr. President." But Ruiz Cortines ordered Olachea to find out whether López Mateos would be interested.

Nevertheless, Olachea assumed that *El Tapado* must be Morones Prieto: Why else would he be held up as the equal of Juárez? The president's request that he check on López Mateos seemed merely an afterthought. But a few days later, when Olachea returned to report that López Mateos was willing to be considered, the president immediately declared, "Now you don't have to go on. That's the one!"

When *El Tapado* assumes office, he becomes the heir of a political structure that is strikingly different from any other in Latin America. The rich entrepreneurs who make up the economic elite are few, and although they exert some influence, they do not manipulate their political counterparts; there is no oligarchy. The military has little political power; the armed forces are small, about 125,000 men, and are kept firmly under civilian control. Nor, in a country that is 89 percent Catholic, does the church heavily influence secular affairs; the clergy is barred by law from voting, owning property, holding public office or commenting on policy.

Priests are forbidden to wear clerical garb in public, or to teach religion to children — even in church schools.

Similarly, the most numerous members of the PRI, the *campesinos,* remain impoverished, poorly educated and virtually powerless. Although some attention is paid them because they provide a major base of voter support for the party, they have so far produced few political leaders to fight convincingly for their concerns.

But the political elite — the government officials, the lawyers and key businessmen, the executives of nationalized industries, the labor leaders and PRI chieftains — make sure they stay on top and are heard, if not always heeded. At one point, when López Portillo planned to raise gasoline prices, Fidel Velázquez, head of the Confederation of Mexican Workers, the nation's largest labor organization, objected to the financial burden this would place on the members. The president reversed his decision on the price increase.

The labor leaders wield extraordinary influence not just on the government, but on those whom they count as followers. Union jobs — prized for the good wages and benefits they offer — are dispensed or withheld by the officials, depending on a worker's willingness to cooperate. Equipped with this weapon, the leaders know that they can threaten strikes or slowdowns with impunity and that the government will go along with their demands.

The most powerful union is the one that, in effect, controls oil, Mexico's biggest and most important industry. When other unions settled for a 20 percent wage increase in 1983, the 120,000 oil workers won a 43 percent raise. Behind this preeminence is a remarkable figure: short, wavy-haired, bespecta-

The shadow of a horseman in a campaign parade falls across a bus emblazoned with the symbol of Mexico's major party, the PRI. The bus was used by the party's presidential candidate on a swing through the country.

Workers from Nanchital arrive in a union bus at the Pajaritos complex for the early-morning shift.

A PATERNAL UNION'S POWERFUL EMBRACE

Whatever employee benefits filter down through the ranks of Mexico's $17-billion petroleum industry arrive by way of the National Oil Workers' Union. With 120,000 members, it is one of the most powerful labor organizations in Mexico. Through its tight control of hiring practices at each job site, the union maintains an overwhelming influence on its members' lives. In return, it has boosted salaries to almost double those in other industries, and as often as not it provides housing, education, entertainment and most of life's other amenities as well.

A model example is Nanchital, a town built by the union in Veracruz for workers at the nearby Pajaritos petrochemical complex. From a modest settlement of adobe huts Nanchital has grown into a city of 30,000 people, with paved streets, running water, bus service, a hospital and a Catholic church — all built and operated under union auspices. And while there is an elected municipal government, the real power rests with the union boss, who dispenses a rich patronage that is the envy of most politicians throughout Mexico.

The boss of Local 11, Francisco Balderas Gutiérrez, confers with a union member at his Nanchital office. Religious memorabilia reflect Balderas' devout Catholicism and his carefully maintained reputation as the town's most upstanding citizen. The TV screens behind his desk monitor the halls, alerting him to who is there.

Outside Balderas' office, oil workers and their families wait hours for a private hearing with the boss, who has power to issue work permits, loans, building lots, student grants, and other favors. As the main source of union patronage, he has behind-the-scenes control over most local affairs.

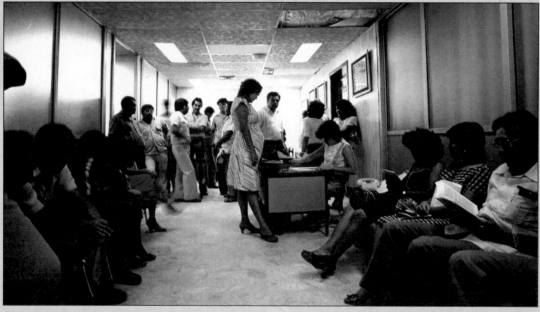

A worker's new house, subsidized by a union loan, goes up in the shadow of an oil storage tank in Nanchital.

A family stocks up on beans, rice and other staples at the union food co-operative, using vouchers paid by the oil company in addition to salary. Another union store nearby sells clothing and discount drugs.

An ornamental kiosk in Nanchital's neatly kept main square sells low-cost sodas and snacks. Behind it rises the proud new Catholic church, built with funds supplied by the union.

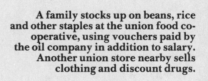

145

Oil workers line up to renew their job contracts at the union office in Pajaritos — a process some of them must repeat every 28 days.

cled Joaquín Hernández Galicia, called La Quina after a contraction of his first name. Officially, he holds a relatively meaningless position in the union hierarchy: Director of Social and Revolutionary Works. But he is, in fact, the boss, ruling firmly and perhaps even ruthlessly. Several of his critics have suggested that it is no coincidence that a number of those who opposed him within the union met thereafter with violent deaths.

"He's not just a gangster — he's a very intelligent manager," said one Mexican oil-industry expert. Through shrewd manipulation, La Quina has built the oil workers' union into a major political force and a financial empire. The union is paid 2.5 percent of its members' wages as dues, but it also has the right to collect 2 percent of the value of contracts awarded to outside companies, the money supposedly to go to "social works." And until 1984, when a new law was enacted, it also had the right to subcontract half of all onshore oil-drilling contracts. According to a former union official, under this arrangement private companies were paying a 35 percent commission to the union for contracts thus awarded. Nevertheless, despite the reforms, the union continues to be involved in some subcontracting.

Much of the union's fortune has been invested in businesses, presumably for the overall benefit of its members. In and around one refinery city, Local 1 of the union owns 16 food and clothing stores; 38,000 acres of ranches and farms; soap, clothing and furniture factories; a metal shop, printing plant and mortuary; construction and trucking companies; a theater; a restaurant; a seaside recreation complex; a health center and a dome-covered sports are-

na. Even the street signs here are labeled "Courtesy of Local 1." How much profit the union derives from all these businesses and exactly who gets what part of it remain moot questions. The union stated that its bank balance in early 1984 came to 15 billion pesos ($90 million).

Labor union chiefs, like the other power brokers, wield some of their national influence through the offices they hold in the PRI. The party is organized almost like a ministry. It is authoritarian in make-up. Decisions are made and policy set at the upper echelons and passed down through a strict hierarchy. PRI members at the higher levels tend also to hold government jobs, and in that capacity, they can find appropriate ears for their arguments and causes. At the same time, members at the grass-roots level have the satisfaction of seeing their requests passed up the pyramid of power to the apex, where they are often acted on.

For the politically ambitious, the PRI offers a route to the top, through the echelons of the government bureaucracy with its 1.5 million employees. The government also happens to be a good place to work. The incomes of those in prominent positions are derived less from their salaries than from the perquisites associated with their jobs — favors, inside information and bribes. Within limits, graft has always been accepted as a part of life in Mexico.

Traditionally, the bureaucrats have been divided into a pair of competing classes: the *políticos,* that is, the elected legislators and the appointed administrators; and the *técnicos,* who are the technical experts.

The *políticos* are professional politicians. But being a politician does not necessarily mean being an elected offi-

147

cial. Echeverría, for example, had held no elected office prior to becoming president in 1970, yet during his career he had mastered the intricacies of the Mexican political system. After marrying into a family prominent in state-level politics and graduating with a law degree from the National Autonomous University of Mexico, he became active in the PRI. Always laboring behind the scenes for his political advancement, he rose to the job of PRI press secretary in 1946 and moved on from there to become a department head first in the Secretariat of the Navy and then in the Secretariat of Education. In 1957 he was named the administrative head of the PRI, and a year later he returned to the government as subsecretary of Internal Affairs. From that position he moved up to secretary, the post he held when he was chosen president.

Echeverría's successors, López Portillo and de la Madrid, were *técnicos*. Although López Portillo had joined the PRI while a university student, he practiced and taught law for a decade before entering the bureaucracy. Unlike Echverría, he held no important posts within the party, and from his entry into government service in 1958 he occupied positions that utilized his skills in planning, investment and management. His last job before becoming president was as finance minister.

The climb to the top by the *técnicos* and *políticos* has been extensively studied by political scientists. "There are no rules," a Mexican kept insisting to Peter H. Smith, Professor of Political Science at the Massachusetts Institute of Technology. Yet in the course of his investigation into Mexican politics, Smith succeeded in isolating 22 different rules of the game. Most would be effective in any country (work hard, don't make enemies), but several have particular application to Mexico:

•Be correctly educated. Three quarters of officeholders have university degrees, and the proportion increases to nearly 90 percent in the upper echelons — in a nation in which less than 4 percent of the population has attended college. But not any school will do. Smith found that during the López Portillo years, 71 percent of the political elite had studied at the president's alma mater, UNAM, and 54.5 percent of them had taught there.

•Affiliate with the PRI. It is not necessary to become an active member, for only a symbolic commitment to the party's egalitarian ideals is important. "Whatever else you do," Smith warned, "do not join an opposition party!"

•Join a camarilla. Every aspiring officeholder seeks membership in a camarilla, an informal group of officials who are loyal to someone higher up in the bureaucracy. Each member's attachment to the camarilla leader must be close enough to curry favor with him, yet not so close as to prevent a successful switch to another patron at the end of the *sexenio,* when tens of thousands of jobs change hands and many leaders find themselves out of power. The game is played by demonstrating public faith in one individual while secretly courting others. "I don't know where I'll be working next week," fretted one 28-year-old bureaucrat shortly before de la Madrid took office. "My patron says he gets along well with the new president, but you never know."

•Take what you can while you can. Self-enrichment through public office "is expected of officials," observed Smith, "and it constitutes a kind of self-protection or insurance against the day when they lose their jobs."

There are different ways of going about this, however, as one former finance minister, Mario Ramón Beteta, revealed to Smith: "I don't know how some people can believe that the minister of finance, the president of the republic, or some other minister can say on one fine day: 'Well, from this or that appropriation of the budget send one half to my home.'

"There are some who believe this, I tell you, there really are. After resigning from the government I personally was accused, for example, of taking the gold reserves of the Bank of Mexico. I say it is absurd, but there are people who believe it.

"There is no need to do it in this way. There are many ways, unethical but legal, that an officeholder can make himself rich. Take, for instance, a public official who knows that a new highway will be constructed and who knows the person in charge of building or directing the project. He can buy, directly or indirectly, the land that will be affected by the highway and thus obtain a profit. Ethically, this is not correct; but legally, it is not a crime.

"On the lower levels of government, as in customs and inspections agencies," Beteta continued, "inspectors do receive what is known in Mexico as a *mordida,* a bribe, a tip for doing or not doing a certain thing. This has various degrees: There is the *mordida* for doing quickly what a person can rightfully request, and this is really a tip; there is the *mordida* for doing something slowly, not rapidly, and this is a serious thing; then there is the third kind of *mordida,* for doing something that a person cannot rightfully request, like letting merchandise into the country without paying duty."

The corruption that Beteta de-

Sparkling lights and an orange gas flare light up the waters around two oil-production stations 50 miles from Ciudad del Carmen, an island in the Bay of Campeche. The water's greenish cast comes from an oil slick.

scribed exists in every country. In Mexico it is pervasive. Many officials who control jobs sell them, pocketing some of the money, passing on the rest to others who must share in the payoffs. An unemployed oil worker told a foreign journalist that the going rate for his type of job was 10 days' pay. "The price is 2,300 pesos (about $100) right now. I'm saving up for it." In 1978 a temporary job lasting two months went for 4,000 pesos, and one lasting three months cost 6,000 pesos. A more or less permanent "general worker" position brought 40,000 pesos; a mechanical-engineering post carried a price tag of 150,000 pesos.

In addition to selling jobs, officials di-vert all kinds of government and industrial property for their own gain and generally get away with it. Moreover, every project, from the building of refineries to the purchase of school supplies, generates commissions for those who issue the contracts. For example, kickbacks to a minor bureaucrat who bought candy for the public schools came to $3,500 a day.

At the upper levels of the government pyramid, cabinet ministers routinely sit on company boards, for which they are well paid; conflict of interest is not generally regarded as an issue. These ministers may also invest as they choose in firms with which they do business, and they can benefit as well from impending legislation and changes in the tariff structure.

According to American political scientist Frank Brandenburg, who has lived and worked in Mexico, in 1964 a cabinet minister who availed himself of ·all the various means of making money could leave the government at the end of a six-year term with two or three houses, perhaps as many automobiles, a good library and $100,000 in cash. A few of the most powerful could depart, Brandenburg suggested, with many times that amount in their pockets.

When corruption is publicly revealed, the Mexican people respond gleefully. Such was the case when the government issued a warrant for the

6

Earth embankments form pools in the salty water of Lake Texcoco outside Mexico City. Here both soda ash and algae are produced. The soda ash is used in making glass, and the algae, which is 70 percent protein, is processed into a food supplement.

arrest of Arturo Durazo Moreno, Mexico City's police chief during the López Portillo years. A former aide accused Durazo of stealing $600 million, a charge the assistant first made in a book that became an instant national bestseller. Durazo — whose official salary came to $65 a week — was able to buy a $2.5-million estate outside Mexico City, complete with heliport, discotheque, gymnasium, private race track, casino, shooting range and artificial lakes. And this was not all. He owned another mansion on the Pacific Coast that was dubbed the Parthenon because of its elaborate columned portico.

Mexican television viewers were treated to tours of these mansions, with the camera zooming in on Durazo's gaudy possessions. A cynical laborer shrugged off the implications: "The first two years they talk about corruption," he said. "The next two years things just go along, and the last two they take what they can."

The effects of graft are felt everywhere. When a house painter who contracted to repaint an apartment was reproached because, weeks later, the work had not begun, he responded, "Oh, señor, it could be done tomorrow if we had a little bit of money to buy paint." A woman applying for a driver's license was asked by the clerk, "With an exam or without an exam?" She chose not to take the exam and wound up paying twice the fee, half of which no doubt went to the clerk. An applicant can even have the eye examination waived, for a fee. In crowded downtown areas of Mexico City, people have learned that paying the local policeman to ignore their double-parked cars all day long is a whole lot cheaper than paying for a private parking space. And anyone involved in a traffic infraction

knows that a policeman will more than likely overlook it, if paid off.

Until recently, it was accepted practice for journalists to take money on the side. Reporters counted for part of their income on payments — *embutes* (sausage stuffing) — from the subjects of their stories. Financial correspondents were paid by bankers, political reporters by politicians. According to one account, even while a high government official was touring the country to denounce corruption and call for "moral renovation," his press officer was passing out the weekly envelopes of *embutes* to the hundred or so accompanying journalists. When the government finally cracked down on such payments, many a reporter's income was halved.

This politico-economic system, based on bribery and cronyism, is regularly deplored and futilely attacked by Mexican leaders. López Portillo began his six-year term — just as Echeverría before him had begun his — by declaring war on corruption. One of the biggest figures to fall was the governor of the state of Coahuila who, rather than face charges of "inexplicable enrichment," resigned. Some said the governor had

enriched himself to the tune of two billion to 10 billion pesos, which at the time would have been worth $80 million to $400 million. On López Portillo's direct orders, half a dozen government officials were jailed, charged with stealing government funds, and in one instance, with extortion. But then the campaign began to fizzle out, and when López Portillo left office, members of his government stood accused of corruption by his successor, de la Madrid, who in turn launched his own "moral renovation" campaign.

Yet in spite of such widespread corruption and the seeming inability of anyone to stop it, Mexico has somehow managed through the years to go on developing. One measure of its progress is its lessening dependence on agriculture as the basis of the economy. About 40 percent of the work force now lives by farming, as compared with 62.4 percent in 1950, and the number is decreasing as industry continues to lure people to the cities.

The shift from agriculture to industry has been abetted by Mexico's rich resources. In addition to plentiful oil, Mexico has abundant silver and sub-

150

stantial deposits of coal, iron, phosphate and sulfur. This natural wealth has allowed the country to set up steel, petrochemical and fertilizer plants.

Mexico boasts some of the most modern steelmaking facilities in the world. Since the end of World War II, production of steel ingots has increased from 260,000 tons per year to more than seven million tons — about equal to East Germany's level.

In manufacturing, Mexico is also among the most advanced of developing nations. It has concentrated on so-called import substitution, that is, on producing domestically many consumer goods that it would otherwise have to import at great cost in foreign exchange. Mexico is accomplishing this by building modern factories for the pro-

duction of consumer goods, then levying tariffs and imposing import restrictions to protect them from foreign competition. To serve its need for cars, Mexico turns out about 300,000 vehicles a year, manufactured by Mexican subsidiaries of American, Japanese and European companies.

A special type of manufacturing for export has sprung up near the United States border. There, relatively unskilled, low-salaried workers assemble — among other things — electronics equipment and household appliances from components made in Asia and North America; the finished products are then shipped out of the country, mostly to the United States.

Together, all types of manufacturing in Mexico — including steel and chemi-

cals, as well as consumer items — make up approximately 25 percent of the value of the country's goods and services, the gross domestic product, compared with 27 percent in Brazil, 29 percent in Italy and 4 percent in that other oil-rich nation, Saudi Arabia.

The industry in Mexico that raises the greatest hopes for the future is, of course, oil. It provided more than 70 percent of the country's export revenues in the mid-1980s, up from scarcely 16 percent in 1976. Indeed, the development of Mexican oil is a tangled story of repeated successes and failures going back to the beginning of the century.

The first oil well began operation in 1901, and by 1921 Mexico was the world's leading oil producer. But by the

Three men stand atop a boxcar being loaded with sulfur, an important ingredient of chemical fertilizers and, for Mexico, a source of foreign exchange. Mexico has the world's fourth-largest sulfur reserves, with an estimated 80 million tons.

151

6

1930s, output had fallen dramatically, partly because of struggles between the Mexican government and foreign oil companies over ownership of the wells. As late as 1973, Mexico was importing oil. Then intensified exploration, aided by new techniques, located a bonanza under the Bay of Campeche, in the southern corner of the Gulf of Mexico. "This is like Saudi Arabia," said drilling rig foreman Procoro Medina. "There they have sand. Here we have water. Underneath, though, we have one thing in common: lakes of oil."

The big discovery was made at a time when worldwide demand for oil was high and prices were about to rise. The government-owned oil monopoly, Pemex, began frenzied expansion to exploit the country's petroleum riches. Between 1977 and 1980 Pemex installed an average of 3.2 miles of pipeline a day, one big compressor every six days, one offshore platform every 19 days, and a new storage tank every three days. By 1982, Pemex employed 134,000 people. Its production is fourth highest in the world today — more than 3 million barrels a day.

The growth in the oil and manufacturing industries set off a welcome boom. Industrial production increased 7 to 8 percent annually between 1978 and 1981. Automobile output alone went up 20 percent a year. Over this period about three million new jobs were created; per capita income rose by nearly 25 percent; and the country's gross domestic product increased about 8 percent annually, a growth rate well ahead of that of the developed nations of the Western world.

But after 1982 Mexico's gross domestic product fell. Hard times, triggered by the decrease in worldwide demand for oil and the correspond-

ing drop in oil prices, were worsened by the country's heavy foreign debt.

Beginning in the early 1970s — before the oil boom — the Mexican government decided to build the economy by investing money borrowed from foreign banks. The borrowing was stepped up to underwrite Pemex when oil exports promised revenues more than sufficient to pay the high interest rates on the loans. That promise soon proved illusory. By 1985 Mexico owed foreign banks $95 billion, a fourth of that debt incurred by Pemex; annual payments on the debt came to $16 billion — payable in dollars, not in pesos. "The money is gone," said a leading American business journal at the time. "It is obvious that Mexico and other developing countries do not have, and never had, the cash-generating capacity to repay the foreign loans they have piled up."

This load of debt had, of course, a devastating effect within Mexico, and to avoid bankruptcy the government imposed severe austerity measures. Prices, interest rates and taxes were raised, pay raises were limited, public spending was slashed, and the value of

the peso — relative to foreign money — was sharply cut. In 1982 the peso plummeted from 26 per dollar to 130 per dollar over a period of barely seven months; in the month of December, inflation, calculated on an annual basis, reached nearly 100 percent. As so many Mexicans feared, the standard of living was hurt, and hurt badly. Interest rates on personal loans rose to 70 percent, government subsidies on basic foods were reduced, gasoline prices tripled and a 15 percent value-added tax was imposed on nonessential items.

The depressed economy refocused attention on Mexico's basic problems, which had persisted despite the years of heady growth in investment, incomes and output. Even though many new jobs had been created during the boom, about 40 percent of the total working population remained underemployed — indeed, for all practical purposes, unemployed. Moreover, much of the increase in earnings had gone to those who were already well off. There was relatively little trickle-down to the mass of the population.

In 1950 the poorest fifth of the population was earning only 4.7 percent of the national income while the richest fifth got 58.9 percent. This inequity steadily worsened. Over the following three decades, the income of the poorest fifth fell to 3.3 percent of the total; and not just the poorest fifth but nearly half of the population suffered a decrease in income share during that period. Even the wealthiest — the top fifth of the population — experienced an income drop; their share declined to 55.1 percent. Only the middle class experienced a gain. The upper middle class increased its share of the national income by 5.2 percent to 41.6 percent, while the lower middle class saw its income rise by 4.5 percent to 28.2 percent of the national total.

As the poor grew poorer, many attempted to leave the country, and the tide of Mexicans entering the U.S. illegally swelled to a flood, with as many as three million people a year crossing the border. The flow, of course, continues. Referred to as "wetbacks" — because some wade or swim across the Rio Grande separating the two countries — most of the immigrants return home after a short stay. Even those who remain as illegal permanent residents send much of their earnings back to their families; an estimated three billion dollars of income is funneled annually into Mexico in this manner.

These remittances — in desperately needed U.S. dollars — have become a crucial underpinning of the Mexican economy. They buy the necessities of daily life for families left behind, and they also help build individual self-sufficiency within Mexico. Some immigrants, returning after their American ventures, take home savings that they invest in farmland or small businesses. One man brought back to his native village in western Mexico enough money to buy two tractors and hire himself out to farmers who needed their land plowed. In the entire region, tilled by some 7,000 people, there were only three other tractors.

Success stories like this are still too rare. The long-term economic impact of Mexico's drive toward modernization remains equivocal. While creating what was once referred to as an economic miracle, Mexican leaders favored industry over agriculture, the urban areas over the rural, the few over the many; and in the process, they almost brought the country to bankruptcy. Yet in terms of social progress there have been gains.

Although Mexico remains an authoritarian, one-party country ruled by an elite, there is increasing opportunity for poor Mexicans to rise into the middle class as social conditions improve, population pressures ease and educational opportunities expand. Mexicans are far healthier than they have ever been before. Steady advances in health care helped to cut the death rate by two thirds between 1940 and 1980. Aver-

age life expectancy, little more than 40 years in 1940, reached the middle 60s by 1980. This was achieved largely through sharp reductions in infant mortality, which dropped by more than half over those four decades (although at 57 per 1,000 in 1980, infant mortality was still eight times the rate in Sweden and Japan, which share the lowest rate in the world).

Increased longevity initially swelled the population figures; between 1940 and 1985 the number of Mexicans nearly quadrupled. For a while, Mexicans were being officially encouraged to have large families. But when the government recognized the economic and social harm unchecked population expansion could do, it began a family-planning campaign in 1972, primarily through education and distribution of contraceptives. Later that year, Mexican bishops took the unusual step of issuing a pastoral letter citing what they called "the very real and excruciating emergency for most Mexican families" brought on by the population explosion and praising the government's family-planning policy as a "humane

6

measure." While the letter adhered to traditional church-supported birth-control techniques, its wording was interpreted by some observers as condoning other methods.

Population growth has slowed, but whether this welcome change is the result of the government family-planning program remains unclear, since birth rates started dropping some years before the program was instituted. Whatever the cause, Mexico claims — perhaps too optimistically — to have its population expansion under control. Growth peaked at about 3.5 percent in 1975 and by 1985 was down to 2.2 percent. The goal is an increase rate of only 1 percent by the end of this century, an objective that may be difficult to achieve. With nearly three quarters of its people under the age of 30, Mexico still faces enormous population growth even if couples limit family size.

One factor now influencing family size is the education level of parents; better-educated couples want fewer children. Interestingly, women who have not gone to school have, on average, six children, but those who have attended college or a professional institution have only 1.3.

In Mexico the number of years children spend in school has increased steadily over recent decades. Although educational opportunities are hardly equal across the country and across social classes, enrollment in primary schools nearly tripled between 1960 and 1980, and university enrollment increased almost 10 times during the same span of time. Literacy, the basic measure of education, has risen from little more than 40 percent in 1940 to 84 percent in 1980.

Partly as a consequence of these social advances, the role of women — in a nation notorious for *machismo* — has expanded. Since the 1970s women have served in the Chamber of Deputies, and others have been appointed to important administrative posts.

These changes are part of a generally freer political atmosphere. The president and the PRI may be supreme, but neither can afford to take dominance for granted. Before each election, the candidate campaigns as if his victory were in doubt. The campaign offers the PRI a chance to reassert its legitimacy and to emphasize its ties to the revolution; at the same time it provides a springboard for local PRI officials wishing to enter the national arena.

During the campaign, the candidate familiarizes himself with the nation's various regions and creates a personal image with the voters. According to his campaign manager, de la Madrid traveled more than 56,000 miles in 1982, visited some 600 cities and villages in 29 states, participated in nearly 2,000 meetings and was seen by at least nine million people. One opposition-party estimate put the cost to the PRI at five billion pesos ($200 million), more than five times the sum spent by the winning party in the United States presidential election two years earlier.

The Mexican president makes visits to areas around the country several times during his term as a way of staying in touch with the people. In a typical village, he will sit in a crowded tent while citizens come to him with requests or complaints — each participant having 30 seconds to make a case. Some people ask for irrigation projects or improvements to a municipal market, others for benefits that seem trivial but are important locally: "two trombones, four trumpets, three saxophones, a drum and a pair of cymbals" to expand the village band, went one request.

The president listens to his petitioners because, however great his power, he needs their support, or at least their acquiescence. Opposition to government action is frequently outspoken and occasionally violent. But gains for the opposition are few. In the 1985 gubernatorial elections in the northern states, voters were expected to show their discontent with the stagnant economy and continuing official corruption. Yet the PRI did not even wait for the polls to close before claiming victory. Charges of stuffed ballot boxes and intimidated voters fell on deaf ears. Said President de la Madrid: "I am not concerned about the confused opinions of the minorities."

Protests also flared up following the September 1985 earthquake in Mexico City, where victims organized marches to decry the government's lack of crisis management and its inefficiency in providing housing and jobs.

The urgent need to deal with Mexico's severe economic problems presents the government's greatest challenge. While Mexico's oil offers the country its greatest hope for a strong economic future, its social inequities present daunting problems that could rend its political fabric. □

In front of the spired and balconied cathedral of Guadalajara, Mexicans belonging to an opposition party hold up a banner demanding "an authentic democracy." The government remains authoritarian, but mild dissent like this is tolerated.

ACKNOWLEDGMENTS

The index for this book was prepared by Barbara L. Klein. For their help in the preparation of this volume, the editors wish to thank the following: John Bailey, Department of Government, Georgetown University, Washington, D.C.; Elizabeth Boone, Curator of the Pre-Columbian Collection, Dumbarton Oaks, Washington, D.C.; Constance Carter, Alexandria, Va.; Kim Conroy, New York; Pilar Franzony de Paul, Press Office, Embassy of Mexico, Washington, D.C.; Philip B. George, Arlington, Va.; Institute of Current World Affairs, Hanover, N.H.; Dennis Kostick, Orlando Martino, Chief, Branch of Latin America and Canada, U.S. Bureau of Mines, Washington, D.C.; Cynthia McClintock, Department of Political Science, George Washington University, Washington, D.C.; Mary Miller, Department of Art History, Yale University, New Haven, Conn.; Susan O'Connor, U.S. Bureau of the Census, Washington, D.C.; Rafael Quijano, Oil Analyst, Petróleos Mexicanos, Washington, D.C.; Steven Sanderson, Department of Political Science, University of Florida, Jacksonville, Fla.; Ing. Mario de la Torre, Cartón y Papel de México, S.A. de C.V., Mexico City; Paul H. Wackworth, U.S. Department of State, Washington, D.C. In addition, these sources were extremely valuable in preparing this volume: *The Discovery and Conquest of Mexico* by Bernal Díaz del Castillo, Farrar, Straus, © 1956; *The Course of Mexican History* by Michael C. Meyer and William L. Sherman, Oxford, 2nd edition, © 1983; *The Mexican Political System* by L. Vincent Padgett, Houghton Mifflin, 2nd edition, 1976; *The Labyrinth of Solitude* by Octavio Paz, Grove Press, © 1961; and *Labyrinths of Power: Political Recruitment in Twentieth Century Mexico* by Peter H. Smith, Copyright © 1979 by Princeton University Press.

PICTURE CREDITS

Credits from left to right are separated by semicolons, from top to bottom by dashes.

Cover: Harald Sund. Front and back endpaper maps: Lloyd K. Townsend. Back endpaper: Digitized by Creative Data, London.

1, 2: Flag Research Center, Winchester, Massachusetts. 6, 7: Thomas Nebbia; chart by Sam Haltom of Another Color, Inc.; Digitized by Creative Data, London. 8, 9: Pedro Meyer; chart by Sam Haltom of Another Color, Inc.; Digitized by Creative Data, London. 10, 11: © Peter Menzel 1983. 12, 13: Graciela Iturbide; chart by Kenneth E. Hancock. 14, 15: Thomas Nebbia; chart by Sam Haltom of Another Color, Inc.; Digitized by Creative Data, London. 16, 17: Graciela Iturbide. 18: © Peter Menzel 1980. 19-21: Thomas Nebbia. 22, 23: © Loren McIntyre — Hiser/Aspen. 24: Pedro Meyer. 25: Graciela Iturbide. 27: © Loren McIntyre. 28, 29: Thomas Nebbia. 30: Hiser/Aspen. 31: © Kenneth Garrett 1983/Woodfin Camp Inc. 32, 33: Graciela Iturbide; Pedro Meyer. 34-36: Pedro Meyer. 37: Pedro Meyer; Graciela Iturbide(2) — Pedro Meyer. 38, 39: Graciela Iturbide, except bottom right, Pedro Meyer. 40, 41: Pedro Meyer; inset, Graciela Iturbide. 42, 43: Tom Jacobi/STERN, Hamburg. 44: © Peter Menzel 1980. 45: Hiser/Aspen. 47: Pedro Meyer. 48, 49: Pedro Meyer(2) — Graciela Iturbide. 50, 51: Pedro Meyer. 52: Graciela Iturbide. 54, 55: Tom Jacobi/STERN, Hamburg. 56, 57: Thomas Nebbia. 58, 59: Steve Northup for *Time*. 61: © René Burri/Magnum, Paris. 62, 63: Graciela Iturbide. 64, 65: Pedro Meyer. 66, 67: Graciela Iturbide(2) — Pedro Meyer(2). 68, 69: Graciela Iturbide. 70, 71: Graciela Iturbide; Pedro Meyer. 72, 73: © Kenneth Garrett 1982/Woodfin Camp Inc. 74: Rare Books and Manuscripts Division, The New York Public Library, Astor, Lenox and Tilden Foundations. 75: Cartón y Papel de México, S.A. de C.V. 76: Irmgard Groth-Kimball/Thames and Hudson Ltd., London. 77: Pedro Meyer. 78, 79: Dumbarton Oaks, Washington, D.C.; © Justin Kerr 1983; Munson-Proctor-Williams Institute, Utica, N.Y.(2); Robert Sonin. 80, 81: Mark Godfrey/© Archive Pictures, Inc. 82: Library of Congress. 84: Cartón y Papel de México, S.A. de C.V. 85: © Norman Prince. 86: © Kenneth Garrett 1982/Woodfin Camp Inc. 88, 89: Private collection, copied by Steve Tuttle; inset, Pedro Meyer. 90-97: Pedro Meyer. 98, 99: © Sebastiao Salgado Jr./Magnum. 100: Melinda Berge/Aspen; David Alan Harvey; Hiser/Aspen. 101: Graciela Iturbide; Thomas Nebbia; Graciela Iturbide. 103: © Bradley Smith/Gemini Smith Inc. 104: Dumbarton Oaks, Washington, D.C.; Library of Congress(3). 105: Library of Congress; Wide World — Pedro Meyer. 107: Library of Congress. 109: Casasola Archives, Mexico City. 110: Library of Congress. 111: Casasola Archives, Mexico City. 112-115: Library of Congress. 116: Casasola Archives, Mexico City. 117: Casasola Archives, Mexico City — UPI. 118, 119: Library of Congress; insets, Casasola Archives, Mexico City. 120, 121: © René Burri/Magnum, Paris. 123: Judith Bronowski. 124, 125: Pierre Kopp, courtesy Museum of Cultural History, Haines Hall at UCLA. 126, 127: © Bradley Smith/Gemini Smith Inc. 128: Painting by Frida Kahlo, *Frieda and Diego Rivera*, 1931, oil on canvas, 39⅜ by 31 in. (100 by 78.7 cm.), San Francisco Museum of Modern Art, Albert M. Bender Collection, Gift of Albert M. Bender, photographed by Don Meyer. 129: Melinda Berge/Aspen. 130: Thomas Höpker/Agentur Anne Hamann, Munich. 132: © Peter Menzel. 133: © René Burri/Magnum, New York. 135: © René Burri/Magnum, Paris. 136, 137: Pedro Meyer. 138: Map by Bill Hezlep; Digitized by Creative Data, London. 140: © Harald Sund. 141: Pedro Meyer. 142, 143: Graciela Iturbide; Pedro Meyer(2). 144, 145: Pedro Meyer(2); Graciela Iturbide. 146, 147: Pedro Meyer. 149: Matthew Naythons for *Time*. 150: Farrell Grehan/Photo Researchers. 151: © Tom McHugh/Photo Researchers. 152: Zigy Kaluzny/Gamma-Liaison. 153: Thomas Nebbia. 155: © Randa Bishop 1983.

BIBLIOGRAPHY

BOOKS

Azuela, Mariano, *Los de Abajo*. New York: Appleton-Century-Crofts, 1939.

Benson, Elizabeth P., *The Maya World*. New York: Thomas Y. Crowell, 1977.

Benítez, Fernando, *The Century after Cortez*. Chicago: The University of Chicago Press, 1965.

Blancké, W. Wendell, *Juárez of Mexico*. New York: Praeger, 1971.

Brandenburg, Frank R., *The Making of Modern Mexico*. Englewood Cliffs, N.J.: Prentice-Hall, 1964.

Bronowski, Judith, *Artesanos Mexicanos*. Los Angeles: Craft and Folk Art Museum, 1978.

Brotherson, Gordon, *The Emergence of the Latin American Novel*. Cambridge: Cambridge University Press, 1977.

Brushwood, John S., *The Spanish American Novel*. Austin, Tex.: University of Texas Press, 1975.

Calvert, Peter:
Emiliano Zapata. London: The Hispanic and Luco Brazilian Council, 1979.
Mexico. New York: Praeger, 1973.

Carrillo Azpeitia, Rafael, *Mural Painting of Mexico*. Transl. by David Casteldine. Mexico City: Panorama Editorial, 1981.

Charlot, Jean, *The Mexican Mural Renaissance*. New Haven, Conn.: Yale University Press, 1963.

Chevalier, François, *Land and Society in Colonial Mexico*. Berkeley, Calif.: University of California Press, 1970.

Coe, Michael D.:
America's First Civilization. New York: American Heritage, 1968.
Mexico. New York: Thames and Hudson, 1982.

Cortés, Hernán, *Letters from Mexico*. New York: Grossman, 1971.

Cosío Villegas, Daniel, et al., *A Compact History of Mexico*. Mexico City: El Colegio de Mexico, 1974.

Cottrell, John, and the Editors of Time-Life Books, *Mexico City* (The Great Cities series). Amsterdam: Time-Life Books, 1979.

Critchfield, Richard, *Villages*. New York: Anchor Press, 1981.

Cumberland, Charles C., *Mexico: The Struggle for Modernity*. New York: Oxford University Press, 1968.

Davies, Nigel, *The Aztecs: A History*. London: Macmillan, 1973.

De la Peña, Guillermo, *A Legacy of Promises*. Austin, Tex.: University of Texas Press, 1981.

Díaz del Castillo, Bernal, *The Discovery and Conquest of Mexico*. New York: Farrar, Straus and Cudahy, 1956.

Eckstein, Susan, *The Poverty of Revolution*. Princeton, N.J.: Princeton University Press, 1977.

The Europa Year Book 1985: A World Survey. London: Europa Publications, 1985.

Fernández, Justino, *A Guide to Mexican Art*. Chicago: University of Chicago Press, 1969.

Foster, David William and Virginia Ramos, *Modern Latin American Literature*. New York: Frederick Ungar, 1975.

Foster, George M., *Tzintzutzan: Mexican Peasants in a Changing World*. New York: Elsevier, 1979.

Goldman, Shifra M., *Contemporary Mexican Paint-*

ing in a Time of Change. Austin, Tex.: University of Texas Press, 1981.

Grayson, George W., *The Politics of Mexican Oil.* Pittsburgh, Pa.: University of Pittsburgh Press, 1980.

Guzmán, Martín Luis, *Memoires of Pancho Villa.* Austin, Tex.: University of Texas Press, 1965.

Harss, Luis, and Barbara Dohmann, *Into the Mainstream.* New York: Harper & Row, 1967.

Hellman, Judith A., *Mexico in Crisis.* New York: Holmes & Meier, 1978.

Helm, MacKinley, *Man of Fire: J. C. Orozco.* New York: Harcourt Brace, 1953.

Herrera, Hayden, *Frida — A Biography of Frida Kahlo.* New York: Harper & Row, 1983.

Johnson, Kenneth F., *Mexican Democracy: A Critical View.* Revised edition. New York: Praeger, 1978.

Johnson, William Weber, *Heroic Mexico.* Garden City, N.Y.: Doubleday, 1968.

Kennedy, Paul, *The Middle Beat.* New York: Teachers College Press of Columbia University, 1971.

Langford, Walter M., *The Mexican Novel Comes of Age.* Notre Dame, Ind.: University of Notre Dame Press, 1971.

Leonard, Jonathan, and the Editors of Time-Life Books, *Latin American Cooking* (Foods of the World series). New York: Time-Life Books, 1968.

Leon-Portilla, Miguel, ed., *The Broken Spears: The Aztec Account of the Conquest of Mexico.* Boston: Beacon Press, 1962.

Levy, Daniel, and Gabriel Székely, *Mexico: Paradoxes of Stability and Change.* Boulder, Colo.: Westview Press, 1983.

Lewis, Oscar, *Anthropological Essays.* New York: Random House, 1970.

Meyer, Karl E., and the Editors of the Newsweek Book Division, *Teotihuacán.* New York: Newsweek, 1973.

Meyer, Michael C., and William L. Sherman, *The Course of Mexican History.* 2nd edition. New York: Oxford University Press, 1983.

Micheli, Mario de, *Siqueiros.* New York: Abrams, 1968.

Nolen, Barbara, ed., *Mexico's People: Land of Three Cultures.* New York: Charles Scribner's Sons, 1973.

Orozco, José Clemente, *José Clemente Orozco: An Autobiography.* Transl. by Robert C. Stephenson. Austin, Tex.: University of Texas Press, 1962.

Padgett, L. Vincent, *The Mexican Political System.* 2nd edition. Boston: Houghton Mifflin, 1976.

Parkes, Henry Bamford, *A History of Mexico.* Boston: Houghton Mifflin, 1966.

Payne, Robert, *Mexico City.* New York: Harcourt Brace, 1968.

Paz, Octavio, *The Labyrinth of Solitude.* Transl. by Lysander Kemp. New York: Grove Press, 1961.

The Phillips Collection, *Rufino Tamayo — Fifty Years of His Painting.* Mount Vernon, N.Y.: Press of A. Colish, 1978.

Quirk, Robert E., *Mexico.* New York: Prentice-Hall, 1971.

Raat, W. Dirk, ed., *Mexico — From Independence to Revolution, 1810-1910.* Lincoln, Neb.: University of Nebraska Press, 1982.

Reed, Alma, *The Mexican Muralists.* New York: Crown, 1960.

Reed, John, *Insurgent Mexico.* New York: Simon and Schuster, 1969.

Robe, Stanley L., *Azuela and the Mexican Underdogs.* Berkeley, Calif.: University of California Press, 1979.

Rodman, Selden, *Tongues of Fallen Angels.* New York: New Directions, 1974.

Rodríguez, Antonio, *A History of Mexican Mural Painting.* New York: G. P. Putnam's Sons, 1969.

Rodríguez Monegal, Emir, ed., *The Borzoi Anthology of Latin American Literature,* Vol. 2. New York: Knopf, 1977.

Rulfo, Juan:
  El Llano en Llamas. Mexico City: Fondo de Cultura Económica, 1953.
  Pedro Páramo. Transl. by Lysander Kemp. New York: Grove Press, 1959.

Sandstrom, Alan R., *Traditional Curing and Crop Fertility Rituals among the Otomí Indians of Sierra de Puebla, Mexico.* Bloomington, Ind.: Indiana University Museum, 1981.

Simpson, Lesley Byrd, *Many Mexicos.* Berkeley, Calif.: University of California Press, 1971.

Smith, Bradley, *Mexico, A History in Art.* New York: Doubleday, 1968.

Smith, Peter H., *Labyrinths of Power: Political Recruitment in Twentieth-Century Mexico.* Princeton, N.J.: Princeton University Press, 1979.

Sommers, Joseph, *After the Storm.* Albuquerque, N. Mex.: University of New Mexico Press, 1968.

Soustelle, Jacques, *Daily Life of the Aztecs.* Stanford, Calif.: Stanford University Press, 1961.

Stuart, Gene S., *The Mighty Aztecs.* Washington, D.C.: National Geographic Society, 1981.

Toneyama, Kojin, *The Popular Arts of Mexico.* New York: Weatherhill/Heibonsha, 1974.

U.S. Bureau of the Census, *Detailed Statistics on the Urban and Rural Population of Mexico: 1950 to 2010.* Washington, D.C.: U.S. Bureau of the Census, 1982.

Weaver, Muriel Porter, *The Aztecs, Maya and Their Predecessors.* 2nd edition. New York: Academic Press, 1981.

Weil, Thomas E., et al., *Area Handbook for Mexico.* 2nd edition. Washington, D.C.: U.S. Government Printing Office, 1975.

Wilkie, James W., and Albert L. Michaels, *Revolution in Mexico: Years of Upheaval, 1910-1940.* New York: Knopf, 1969.

Wolfe, Bertram D., *The Fabulous Life of Diego Rivera.* New York: Stein and Day, 1963.

PERIODICALS AND OTHER SOURCES

Bermúdez, José Y., "A Word with Tamayo." *Américas,* August 1974.

"Can Mexico City Survive?" *Encuentro,* Mexico City *News,* September 1, 1983.

"The Capital of Underdevelopment." *Harper's,* May 1981.

Chereny, Lawrence, and Manuel Bennett, "Dr. Atl: Father of Mexican Muralism." *Américas,* February 1981.

Conroy, Kimberly A., "Chiapas Revisited." (KAC 18) Institute of Current World Affairs, April 21, 1983.

"Dying an Urban Death?" San Jose *Mercury,* August 20, 1983.

Eberstadt, Nick, "La Crisis." *The New Republic,* October 18, 1982.

Edwards, Mike, "Mexico: A Very Beautiful Challenge." *National Geographic,* May 1978.

Gall, Norman, "Can Mexico Pull Through?" *Forbes,* August 15, 1983.

Green, Eleanor Broome, "Tamayo: The Enigma and the Magic." *Américas,* March 1979.

"The Growing Pains of Mexico's Biggest Slum." Dallas *Times-Herald,* March 9, 1980.

International Labor Review, "The Place of Mexico City in the Nation's Growth: Employment Trends and Policies." May-June 1982.

"Mexican Child Rearing Fights Macho Tradition." *Christian Science Monitor,* June 19, 1978.

"Mexican Feminists Turn Their Attention to Social Issues." *The New York Times,* December 12, 1979.

"Mexico: Art and Activism." *Newsweek,* July 27, 1964.

"Mexico: Crisis of Poverty/Crisis of Wealth." *The Los Angeles Times,* July 15, 1979.

"Mexico Has Created a Monster Too Big, Too Dirty, Too Poor." *The Miami Herald,* February 26, 1981.

"Mexico's Oil Workers Have Powerful Leader in Hernandez Galicia." *Wall Street Journal,* January 20, 1984.

"Mexico's Unfolding Graft: A Prodigal Police Chief." *The New York Times,* January 31, 1984.

"Mexico, the City That Founded a Nation." *National Geographic,* May 1973.

"Mexico: Turmoil and Promise." *Christian Science Monitor,* April 5, 1979.

Nicholson, H. B., "Revelation of the Great Temple." *Natural History,* July 1982.

Population Reference Bureau, "Mexico's Population Policy Turnaround." December 1978.

"Problems of Mexico City." *The New York Times,* May 15, 1983.

Riding, Alan, "Facing the Reality of Mexico." *The New York Times Magazine,* September 16, 1980.

Sanders, Thomas G., "Mexican Population: 1982." *Universities Field Staff Reports* 1982/No. 34.

Shorris, Earl, "Homage to Juan Rulfo." *The Nation,* May 15, 1982.

"The Squatter Settlement as Slum or Housing Solution: Evidence from Mexico City." *Land Economics,* August 1976.

Squirru, Rafael, "Tamayo: Mexican par Excellence." *Américas,* October 1963.

U.S. Dept. of Energy, Energy Information Administration, "The Petroleum Resources of Mexico." (Foreign Energy Supply Assessment series.) Washington, D.C., 1983.

Vasquez, Juan M., "Mexico City: Strangling on Growth." *The Los Angeles Times,* December 8, 1983.

"We are in an emergency." *Time,* December 20, 1982.

"Women in the Informal Labor Sector: The Case of Mexico City." *Signs,* The Journal of Women in Culture and Society, autumn 1977.

rededication, 80; sacrifices at, 82; sculptures, *72-73, 86*
Guadalajara: cathedral, *155;* Orozco's work in, 131, *132*
Guanajuato, *6-7*
Gutiérrez Baez, Javier, 56
Guzmán, Martín Luis, 133

H

Hacendados (plantation owners), 26
Health, improvements in, 153
Hernández Galicia, Joaquín (La Quina), 147
Hidalgo y Costilla, Miguel, 102, *103, 132*
Highland plateau, 19
History and historical figures, 99-115; agriculture, 22-23, 26; chaos, post-independence, 106; chronology, *104-105;* colonial period, 99-102; constitution (1857), 106; constitution (1917), 23, 114, 115; Díaz, Porfirio, 105, 107, 108, 109, 110; independence movement (1810-1821), 102-103; Juárez, Benito, *105,* 106, 107, 108; Madero, Francisco, *98, 109,* 110, 111; Maximilian, 106-108; Mexican revolution (1910-1920), 105, 109-*110,* 111-112, *112-113,* 114, 115, 116, *117-119;* Obregón, Alvaro, 105, 111, 112, 114, *115;* social structure of New Spain, 100-102; Villa, Pancho, *98-99,* 105, 111, 112, *113,* 114-115, *119,* 133; Zapata, Emiliano, *99,* 111, 112, 114, *116, 119. See also* Ancient civilizations
Hotel de Mexico, Mexico City, Sequeiros mural in, 128-129, *130*
Huave Indian, *101*
Huerta, Victoriano, 110-111, 112
Huitzilopochtli (Aztec god), 76, 77, 80
Human sacrifices, Aztec, 80, *82*

I

Ignacio Amor, José, quoted, 57
Illegal entrants into United States, 31, *152,* 153
Import substitution, 151
Income, inequities in, 152-153
Independence Day celebrations, 60, *62-63*
Independence movement (1810-1821), 102-103
Indians, 20, *68, 100-101;* in colonial period, 101; under Díaz regime, 108-109; miners, *107;* Otomí, *8-9, 89-97, 101;* Zapotec, *24-25, 101. See also* Ancient civilizations
Industrial pollution, 56
Industry, 150-152; Mexico City, 45; oil, *chart* 12, *12-13, 105, 142-143, 148-149,* 151-152; railroads and, 108; shift to, from agriculture, *chart* 15, 150; tourism, 11
Iturbide, Agustín de, 103, 104, 106

J

Jaguar in ancient art, 75
Jaina (island), Mayan figurines from, *78-79*
Job mart in Mexico City, 53, *56*
Jobs: government, 147, 148; Mexico City, 45, 53, *57;* selling of, 149
Journalists, payments to, 150
Juárez, Benito, *105,* 106, 107, 108; bust of, *120*
Juchitán, market in, *14-15*

K

Kahlo, Frida, 122, 123, 126; in mural, *129;* painting by, *128*

L

Labor unions, 141, 142, 147; office, *146-147;* town built by, 142, *143-145*
Labyrinth of Solitude (Paz), 134
Laguna region, *ejido* program in, 26
Lajous, Adrian, 137
Land laws, Díaz legislature's, 108
Language, 18
Latin American Tower, Mexico City, 59
Lerdo de Tejado, Sebastián, 108
Life expectancy, increased, 153
Literature and literary figures: Azuela, Mariano, 133; Fuentes, Carlos, 133-134; Guzmán, Martín Luis, 133; Paz, Octavio, 18-19, 134; Rulfo, Juan, 134-135
Loans, foreign, 152
Locomotive, wrecked, *118-119*
López, José, quoted, 31
López Mateos, Adolfo, 141
López Portillo, José, 137-138, 139, 141, 148; war on corruption, 150

M

Macho, 18-19
Madero, Francisco, *98, 109,* 110, 111
Manufacturing, 151
Maps: of oil reserves, *138;* 16th century, of Tenochtitlán, *74*
March of Humanity on Earth toward the Cosmos, The (Siqueiros), 128-129, *130*
Marín, Guadalupe, 122, 123
Marina, Doña (Indian princess), 74, *75*
Market day in Coyoacán plaza, *68-69*
Marketplaces: Aztec, 83-84; Juchitán, *14-15*
Martínez, Herón, work of, *124*
Marxist, Rivera as, 123, 126
Mass transit in Mexico City, 57, 60
Matadors, aspiring, *36-37*
Maximilian (Ferdinand Maximilian Josef), 106-108
Mayas (Indians), 75-76; city (Palenque), *77;* clay figures, *78-79;* present-day, *100*
Medina, Procoro, quoted, 152
Medrano, Candelario, work of, *125*
Mendez Gonzales, Esteban, 46
Mestizos (persons of mixed blood), 101, *107*
Mexican Renaissance, defined, 121
Mexican revolution (1910-1920), 105, 109-*110,* 111-112, *112-113,* 114, 115, 116, *117-119;* as artistic inspiration, 121, 133-134; celebration of, *98-99*
Mexico City, 43-60; aerial views, *42-45, 58;* air pollution, 55-56, *58;* appearance of people, 43; boulevards, 43-*44;* crime, 59; crowding, 44, 59; as cultural center, 43; decentralization, 60; jobs and workers, 45, 53, *56,* 57; middle class, 53, 55; migrations to, 31, 44-45; National Palace, *140;* Olympic Summer Games (1968), *105;* slums and slum dwellers, 45-46, *47-52,* 53, *54-55;* subsoil, unstable, 59, 60; Sunday in, 43; transportation problems

and solutions, 56-57, *59,* 60; water and sewage, 59; Zapatistas, *111;* Zócalo (plaza), 17, 60
Middle class, Mexico City's, 53, 55
Mijangos Muñoz, Juan, and family, *47-52*
Minatitlán, *12-13*
Miners, silver, *107*
Ministry of Public Education murals, Rivera's, 123
Moctezuma I (Aztec emperor), 77, 80
Moctezuma II (Aztec emperor), 80-81, 82-83, *84,* 85, 86
Moon-goddess, Mayan, figures of, *78-79*
Mordida (bribe), 148
Morelos, José María, 102, 103
Mother Earth, Rivera's figure of, 123, *126-127*
Motozintla, popular protest in, 154
Mountains, 19
Murals: by Orozco, 130-131, *132;* by Rivera, 122-123, *126-127, 129;* by Siqueiros, 128-129, *130*
Musicians, *70-71*

N

Nahua Indian, *100*
Nahual (guardian spirit) figure, *125*
Nanchital, 142, *143-145*
Napoleon III, emperor (France), 106, 107
Nationalization of banks, 137-138
National Oil Workers' Union, 141, 142, 147; office, *146-147;* town built by, 142, *143-145*
National Palace, Mexico City, *140*
National Preparatory School, Mexico City, murals painted in: by Orozco, 130-131; by Rivera, 122-123; by Siqueiros, 128
Natural resources, 22, 150; fish, *24-25;* silver, production of, *chart* 6, 107
Negrete, María Eugenia, quoted, 59
Nezahualcóyotl, Ciudad, 46; inhabitants, *47-52;* sculpture, *120*
Nobility, Aztec, 81
Nuns, *64*

O

Obregón, Alvaro, 105, 111, 112, 114, *115*
Ochoa, Raúl E., quoted, 59
Offshore oil-production stations, *149*
Oil, 22; fields, *map* 138; industry, *chart* 12, *12-13, 105, 142-143, 148-149,* 151-152
Oil workers' union, 141, 142, 147; office, *146-147;* town built by, 142, *143-145*
Olachea Aviles, Agustín, 141
Olmec civilization, 75; statuary, 75, *76, 104*
Olympic Summer Games (1968), *105*
Orozco, José Clemente, 122, 129-131; Guadalajara, work in, 131, *132*
Otomí Indians, *8-9, 89-97, 101*
Ox-drawn cart, *27*

P

Painters, lives and works of: folk painting, *103;* Orozco, José Clemente, 122, 129-131, *132;* Rivera, Diego, 122-123, *126-129;* Siqueiros, David Alfaro, 122, 127-129, *130;* Tamayo, Rufino, 131-*133*

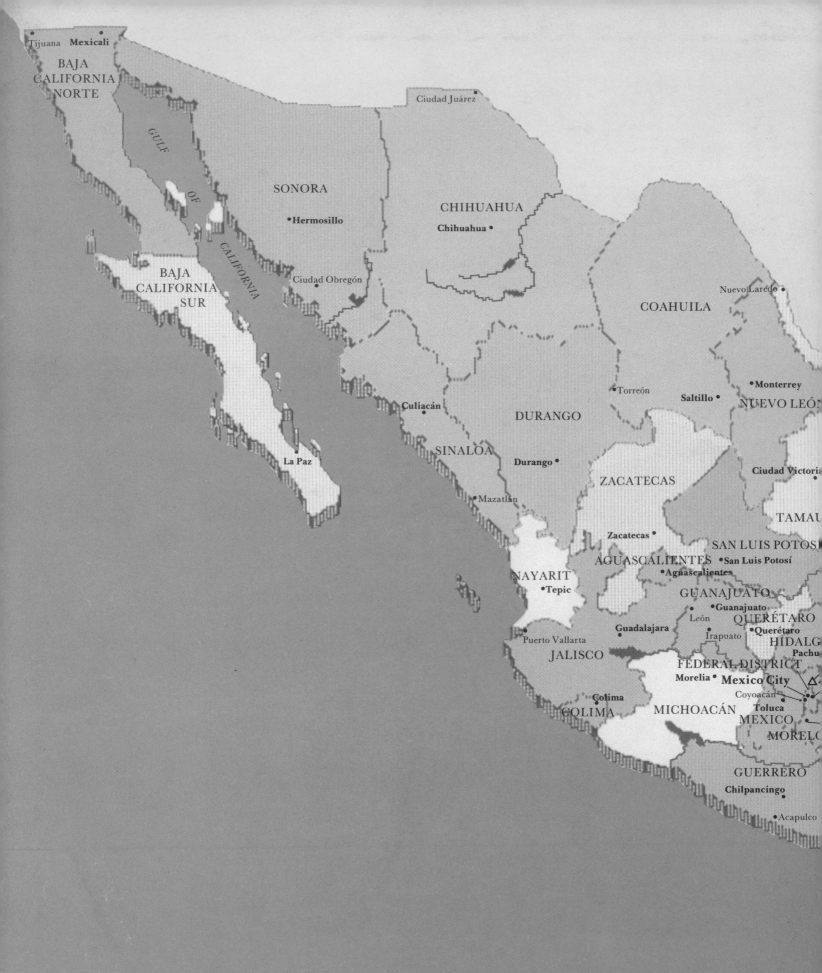

Tijuana   **Mexicali**

BAJA CALIFORNIA NORTE

GULF

OF

CALIFORNIA

Ciudad Juárez

SONORA

• **Hermosillo**

CHIHUAHUA

Chihuahua •

Ciudad Obregón

BAJA CALIFORNIA SUR

Nuevo Laredo •

COAHUILA

Torreón •

• **Monterrey**

Saltillo •

NUEVO LEÓN

Culiacán •

DURANGO

SINALOA

Durango •

La Paz •

Ciudad Victoria

ZACATECAS

Mazatlán •

TAMAU

Zacatecas •

SAN LUIS POTOSÍ

AGUASCALIENTES

• **San Luis Potosí**

• **Aguascalientes**

NAYARIT

• **Tepic**

GUANAJUATO

• **Guanajuato**

León •

QUERÉTARO

Irapuato •

• **Querétaro**

Guadalajara •

HIDALG

Pachu

Puerto Vallarta •

JALISCO

FEDERAL DISTRICT

Morelia •

• **Mexico City**

Coyoacán •

• **Colima**

Toluca

MICHOACÁN

MEXICO

COLIMA

MORELO

GUERRERO

Chilpancingo

• Acapulco